WRITING FROM SCRATCH
The Essay

by
John Clark Pratt

Hamilton Press

Lanham • New York • London

Copyright © 1987 by

Hamilton Press

4720 Boston Way
Lanham, MD 20706

3 Henrietta Street
London WC2E 8LU England

Printed in the United States of America

British Cataloging in Publication Information Available

Library of Congress Cataloging-in-Publication Data

Pratt, John Clark.
  The essay.

  (Writing from scratch)
  1. English language—Rhetoric. 2. Exposition
(Rhetoric) I. Title. II. Series.
PE1429.P7 1987   808'.042   87-12087
ISBN 0-8191-5444-X (alk. paper)
ISBN 0-8191-5445-8 (pbk. : alk. paper)

All Hamilton Press books are produced on acid-free
paper which exceeds the minimum standards set by the National
Historical Publication and Records Commission.

Table of Contents

For Sandy,
a book she can read

Author's Preface

YOU'RE ABOUT TO START A BOOK that will be different from anything you've read, and by the time you finish, you should have a good understanding of how a piece of expository writing is conceived, structured, written, revised, and rewritten for completeness and excellence. I also hope that you'll enjoy reading *Writing from Scratch*.

Are you in college? In the work force? In high school? Retired? In business management? In sales? I don't know, of course, but what you do for a living is less important than the fact that you want to write better. This book should help you much as my method has helped the more than 1000 writing students I've taught during my college teaching career.

What I'm about to show you is how to put together an essay—and I'm going to do so by having you watch me work, suffer, and struggle with the writing process. When I started *Writing from Scratch*, I did not know what I was going to write about in my sample essay, but during the creation of this book, I decided to compose a personal essay—one that ended up a little more personal than I'd at first intended.

A *personal* essay? I can hear some of my editorial and academic colleagues snicker. Perhaps you have taken a class from one of them or read one of their books: you know, the sanitized, by-the-numbers writing approach that tells you how to write for a particular discipline, or how to structure an essay in each mode of discourse, or how to write an "argument" with a "purpose."

I don't knock these approaches; I just think that most of them don't start at the beginning, from *scratch*, as I try to do here. If you can write a good personal essay, you can, with an understanding of a few additional guidelines (how to do charts, graphs, tables; how to use more advanced stylistic, linguistic, and rhetorical devices), write anything at all—and do it well. *Writing from Scratch* will provide you with all the necessary basics for any piece of expository writing you will ever have to do.

Even Argument? Of course. I believe that *all* writing is argument, that even a laboratory report argues that what the writer is saying is correct, that even a primarily descriptive paper argues that its creator is describing accurately, that even an analytic study attempts to persuade the reader that its conclusions are true. There are, of course, many advanced methods of presenting argumentative ideas, but these matters are for writers who have first learned to write satisfactorily about anything—from scratch.

Also, you should note two other characteristics of this book: first, I don't talk about writing on the word-processor or computer; and second, I'm going to sound quite dictatorial at times. I like computers (I'm fascinated, for instance, with interactive fiction). I've taught composition on computers for years, but I'm discovering that writers who depend wholly on a word processor often have problems similar to those mathematics students who have always depended only upon a calculator. There is *process* involved both in mathematics and writing that requires one to see the *whole,* not merely one part at a time, whether that part be a numerical LED display or a paragraph on a video screen. (You've noticed, I'm sure, how the calculator manufacturers have moved away from the display-only machines and are now marketing compact printers as well.)

By all means use a word-processor or home computer, but *print out as you go along* so that you can refer back to page 3 and page 5, for instance, when you're writing page 10. When you have your first draft printed, revise as I'll show you in Chapter 7; then do a final draft and edit with any of the software available to you. I don't advise at all trying to go from rough to final draft without printing, because even with a split-screen display, you can look only at two small portions of your essay at once—and too often much like the calculator total (from your checkbook, for instance) that comes out wrong, so too can an essay end up badly unless you have constant access to every line you've put into it. So adapt, but don't ignore, the traditional writing process that I'll be showing you here.

Finally, about my being dictatorial: I'm not an ogre (as I think you'll see from my essay), but I do think that the best way to help you learn how to write is to push and pull you in the direction that I've learned will work. In addition to writing, I've taught many other skills—skiing, flying, fishing, and driving (I have a old car that shows dents added by each of my children)—and I believe strongly that in order to learn how to do something yourself, you should first understand exactly how someone *else* does it. Sure, I'm a professional writer, but the major difference between me and you is simply that I've been at this business of writing a lot longer than you have. I'm probably better at it only because I started sooner, and I hope that as a result of this book, you'll learn enough basic techniques to enable you to progress much further in your chosen field than you otherwise might.

John Clark Pratt

law: all the rules of conduct . . .
having to do with a
particular sphere of
human activity.
Webster's *New World
Dictionary*

Chapter 1

The Basic Law of Good Writing

TO ACHIEVE GOOD WRITING SKILLS, you should start now by learning, understanding, and obeying the Basic Law of Good Writing. I mean "obey." If you do so, you'll write well. If you don't, you'll continue to muddle along as you probably have: worrying, wasting time, asking for help you wish you didn't need, and stumbling toward last minute completion of that report, essay, or other writing project.

Not only should you never break this law, but you must also realize that you are its primary enforcer. Although failure to comply will not cause fines, warnings, or jail terms, what will probably happen is that your supervisor or teacher will keep on making those comments that you've so often heard: "Not a bad start. . . . There are some interesting possibilities. . . . Too bad you didn't have more time." You'll also keep feeling that familiar prickling flush of inadequacy that accompanies your realization that yes, you certainly could have done better.

If you'll apply this Basic Law of Good Writing to everything

1

you write from now on, I doubt if you'll hear these kinds of comments again. Study this Law; memorize it; and adapt it to all future writing. If you doubt that the Law applies, show it to anyone with experience in submitting or receiving written communications and watch that person agree.

As are most laws, this one is synthetic.[1] A product of writing techniques discussed in most handbooks, manuals, and guides, the Basic Law of Good Writing defines the method used by most effective writers. Many professionals consciously follow each of the Law's nine steps; others comply instinctively because of their practical experience. Like the law of gravity, however, you can be certain that this law works.

Each of the nine components of the Basic Law of Good Writing illustrates a specific step—from conception to completion—of the writing process. Here is the Law:

> SUBJECT
>
> TOPIC
>
> LIMITED TOPIC
>
> THESIS and THESIS STATEMENT
>
> OUTLINE
>
> ROUGH DRAFT
>
> REVISED DRAFT
>
> FINAL DRAFT
>
> PROOFREADING

As you'll discover, the development of *Writing from Scratch* itself illustrates this Law. Here are some brief definitions:

SUBJECT [Chapter 2]

The general, abstract area into which not only your writing project but also many others fit. Examples: Love, Religion, Science, Human Rights, Personnel Management, Ecology, War, ————————————, or ————————————.

---

[1]No effective writer is without a dictionary within reach. Please get one. Use it when you encounter *any* word—when you are reading or writing—that you can't define specifically in the context in which it is being used. Make certain that you know how I am using "synthetic" here.

TOPIC [Chapter 2]

A narrowing of the Subject area, but still too general for effective treatment in a writing project. Examples (derived from the
above Subjects): High School Romance; Roman Catholicism;
Nuclear Energy; Freedom of Speech; Supervisor-Employee
Relations;   Water   Pollution;   The   Vietnam   War;
_____, or _____.

LIMITED TOPIC [Chapter 2]

A further narrowing, and if you're lucky, *possibly* a topic specific
enough to write about. Examples: One's First Serious Romance;
The Issue of Priestly Celibacy; Fossil vs. Nuclear Energy; Contemporary Applications of the First Amendment to the United
States Constitution; How to Write Annual Employee Perform-
ance Reports; Dealing with Industrial Waste; The Use of Air-
power in the Vietnam War; _____, or
_____.

Stop, please.

Look at the above three steps. Something interesting happens
when a Subject is limited. Look at "Science," for instance, as this
one word becomes narrowed to the Limited Topic of "Fossil vs.
Nuclear Energy" (four words). When you are determining exactly
what it is that you should write *about*, the more you limit during
your planning process, the more you will be able to say. Try this
limiting process yourself: in the blank spaces above, fill in two
Subjects, Topics, and Limited Topics of your choice; or use one of
the given Subjects and create more specific Topics and Limited
Topics. Be certain that each of your entries derives from and
represents a narrowing of its antecedent.[2]

---

[2]Another dictionary exercise. From now on, I won't always asterisk words you
should look up. Know what this word means in its grammatical sense.

THESIS and THESIS STATEMENT [Chapter 3]

Your writing project's basic intention, stated in a single sentence which gives direction to your work. Often arrived at during the next step, Outlining, the Thesis Statement may or may not appear in your Final Draft. Here are two examples of Thesis Statements:

> The United States should depend more upon coal than upon Nuclear Energy because coal is so plentiful, so much cheaper to process, and so much safer to use.

> Employees should always be shown their annual performance ratings because doing so keeps the lines of communication open, permits them to assess their own performance in relation to that of their peers, and results in better overall productivity.

OUTLINE [Chapter 4]

The basic plan for your writing project. Don't believe *anyone* who says that an outline—in *some* form—is not always required. Writing an essay without an outline is like building a house without using a blueprint or baking a cake without consulting a recipe.

ROUGH DRAFT [Chapter 5]

Your first actual *writing*, characterized by its strike-overs, errors, juvenile sentences, and statements you wish you'd never made. In comparison with the Final Draft, the Rough Draft resembles your spouse—ten seconds after the alarm clock buzzes in the morning. This draft *must* be double or triple spaced.

REVISED DRAFT [Chapter 7]

In appearance, a mutilation of your Rough Draft after you have added and deleted words and sentences or moved sections around (often with the aid of scissors and plastic tape).

FINAL DRAFT [Chapter 7]

The finished product, properly typed or neatly handwritten. This Final Draft should be copied from your Revised Draft with *very few* changes. Looking at your final draft immediately after completing it, you will be certain that your project needs no further work. You're wrong. If possible, put your Final Draft in a drawer and do something else for at least four hours.

PROOFREADING [Chapter 7]

The last step of the writing process that lets your reader know how much pride you take in your work. Failure to proofread properly is like chewing gum during a job interview.

Here, with some modifications, is the Basic Law again:

SUBJECT

TOPIC

LIMITED TOPIC, etc., etc., etc. . . . .

THESIS and THESIS STATEMENT

OUTLINE

ROUGH DRAFT

REVISED DRAFT

FINAL DRAFT

PROOFREADING

Know this Law. The etceteras that follow Limited Topic indicate the frequent need to continue the limiting process through many stages, depending upon the scope of your project. For instance, the Limited Topic "Fossil vs. Nuclear Energy" is much too general for anything but a lengthy book. "How to Adapt Your Furnace to Coal," however, is a further topic limitation that could be handled in a relatively short paper. As you'll see demonstrated later, the limiting process never really stops.

Also, the arrows which link Thesis Statement and Outline show that these two steps in the writing process are often accomplished at roughly the same time. You may not have decided upon your actual Thesis Statement before starting your outlining process; or while structuring your project, you may find that your original Thesis just won't work and needs to be changed. Always be alert for this possibility.

Look again at the Basic Law of Good Writing. Considered individually, each step is a specific requirement for any writing project. Seen as a whole, however, this Law presents the sequential pattern for effective writing.

Do any of these requirements bother you? What about the need for *two* drafts? For a written Thesis Statement? For the apparent rigidity of it all? Or for the apparent *time* that following the Law might take?

Please don't worry, especially about time. Once you learn how to use this Law, you will *save* time. More important, you will learn to use your available time much more productively. No one can promise that you will immediately start writing feature articles for national publications, but your writing will be better. You'll notice the improvement, and more important, so will everyone else.

Chapter 2

Conceiving

===

Beginning

WHEN I FIRST BEGAN WRITING REQUIRED PAPERS, I was often afflicted by the "blank page syndrome." You've experienced it, I know. Your boss or instructor has requested a report or a paper by the following Tuesday, and seated at a desk, you glance first at a white piece of paper in front of you, then at the clock. You take a pen or pencil in hand or put a fresh sheet in your typewriter. Nothing happens. After about five minutes, you conclude that you have plenty of time after all, so you decide to do something else. Perhaps you make a note on your calendar; perhaps you merely decide to get back to your project "later." You might even think that your idea to improve sales efficiency or reduce overhead might not ever work, so you make a phone call, take a coffee break, or go to a movie—*anything* to keep from violating the pristine whiteness of that untrammeled piece of paper. Often, the result of the blank page syndrome is that on Monday night you are once again at the same desk with the same blank page and the same clock, but now you can see the hands of

7

the clock move and you feel as if you're developing a rash and
fever.

Here are some practical suggestions to counter this syndrome.
First, don't ever use white paper for preliminary work. I use
yellow legal pads, and at this moment I am staring at some notes I
jotted some time ago for this chapter. Under the heading "Subjects, Topics, Limited Topics" (written in pencil) I later added the
following in black ink: "1. Free. 2. Assigned. Consider a note on
Research." Then there are three blank lines before the next entry.
The rest of the yellow page is a mess: lines crossed out, numbers
all over the place, arrows, and some comments which I can't quite
make out. This yellow page is wrinkled from having been folded
once or twice, and the bottom left corner is torn off.

This page *looks* like a rough beginning, the first part of what
publishers call the "foul matter" of a finished work. Your initial
notes should look just as nondescript. There is nothing I know
that more successfully delays completion of a project than a white
piece of paper with three or four neatly written introductory
sentences. This "opening" usually has a final sentence that has
been either crossed out or is unfinished because the writer ran out
of ideas or became distracted. Each time one returns to this
project, its aborted beginning tells the author that there has
already been one of many failures.

So start with a yellow sheet, lined or unlined, and write down
the general instructions which govern your project; then record
the desired approximate length in number of words or pages.
Obviously, the overall length of your project will be a function of
the time you can spend on it, so do some rough figuring. How
many clock hours can you realistically devote to writing? How
many pages do you think you can produce in that time? Write
down these numbers, too. You should know that no good project
can be accomplished if a writer misjudges matters of time and
space. If you have twenty working hours for your project, for
instance, you obviously cannot write a book, but you might be able
to do a reasonably impressive 2,000 word paper, depending upon
the amount of research needed.[1]

After determining how much time you have and approxi-

---

[1] I have just crossed out the phrase "Note on Research" on my yellow note
page. The present plan for this book is to make it short; therefore, I'll omit a
discussion of research techniques. The subject is just too big for *Writing From
Scratch*. When you work on your own material, you should make the same kind
of decisions, difficult as they may seem, as you go along.

mately how extensive your project is to be, use either a manila folder or a large spring clamp to hold your foul matter. I prefer the clamp, because I can then hang the pages on the corkboard over my desk. As a result, my unfinished project is always there glaring at me until I take it down and do some more work on it. The folders I once used at this stage of writing seemed too easily to escape into bottom drawers.

By doing these few mechanical beginning chores, you will have effected a transition from the thought to the *act* of writing, and you are ready to begin.

The Limiting Process

A paper's Subject, defined in Chapter 1 as "The general, abstract area into which . . . your writing project . . . fits," originates in one of two ways: either it is assigned to you; or you conceive it yourself. Many beginning writers prefer an assignment, such as "Do a paper on the Breakdown of Mexican-American Relations before the Civil War." Writing is easier, some say, when you are told what to write about.

Don't believe a word of this myth. Writing is never easy, but regardless of Subject, if you select the right Limited Topic you will better be able to achieve what I think should be your overall goal: to write well about something important.

Therefore, you should understand that writing about an assigned or "free" Subject requires exactly the same procedure, and the Basic Law applies in either case. The key is proper limiting, and as I'll show later, you will often be able to make all of the world-shaking points you want to make, while at the same time write an essay which has the crispness of a fresh salad and the sting of wind blown salt air.

What do I mean by "proper limiting"? In *Zen and the Art of Motorcycle Maintenance,* a book which is about neither zen nor motorcycles but about the quality of life, Robert Pirsig tells this story: a student of his, a young woman who "wanted to write a five-hundred-word essay about the United States," soon became convinced that she had nothing to say. The deadline for her paper arrived. Pirsig's attempts to persuade her to limit her subject, first to the town in which she lived, then to the main street of that town, all failed. She just could not think of anything to say. Finally, Pirsig ordered this student who he claimed had shown no creativity at all, "Narrow it down to the *front* of *one* building on the main street. . . . The Opera House. Start with the upper left hand brick."

At the next class period, the student handed in an essay. Writing about that first brick, she said, had led to writing about the second, then the third—and she found that she could not stop. By deciding to write just about that first brick, Pirsig concludes, the student was forced "to do some original and direct seeing"—and the result was a 5000-word essay of definite quality.[2]

From now on, whenever you write anything, *remember Pirsig's brick.* By limiting your Topic as much as you possibly can, you will create not only something to write *about* but also will insure that your project has focus as well. Consider the last sunset photograph you took; you focussed your camera on *one* scene, *one* selection of shapes and colors. By limiting to that one place at that one time, however, you managed to show how beautiful *all* Nature can be.

How do you discover just the right brick for a particular writing project? Often, you'll trip over it during the conceiving or planning process. You'll rarely start off with the right Limited Topic in mind. You should begin by creating *many* possible Limited Topics; then discard all but one. To start the limiting process, take that same piece of yellow paper and write down anything which occurs

[2]Robert M. Pirsig, *Zen and the Art of Motorcycle Maintenance,* new edition, New York: Bantam, 1968, pp. 170–71. I have just written *stet* opposite the crossed-out phrase "Note on Research" on my yellow note sheet for this chapter. *Stet* is proofreader's Latin for "let it stand." During the drafting of any work, you'll change your mind often. Here is a brief "Note on Research" documentation techniques.

As exemplified by the above citation of Pirsig's work, the general rules for writing footnotes and bibliography are basically the same: always list the Author's name, the Title of the work, and the Facts of publication (city, publisher, date). Titles are written in quotation marks if the work is little (an essay, article, poem, short story); if the work cited is big (a novel, a textbook, a collection of essays), the title is underlined. Footnotes use commas throughout; bibliography entries use periods. For footnotes, start with the author's first name, but in bibliographies, start with the author's *last* name. Why the difference? It's the way most people do it, that's why. For specialized footnote and documentation techniques, each profession has its own preferred style manual. Ask your instructor or someone in your Public Relations/Communications Office. If these people can't tell you which style manual you should use, then they don't know as much as they should know about their jobs.

Finally, *always* give proper documentary credit for someone else's words or ideas. Always.

to you which seems relevant to your project. Don't try to achieve focus; just *write*.

Free Subjects

If the choice of Subject is yours, write down anything at all that is important to you, the more general the better. Make a list of words or phrases, and space each concept at least three lines apart. Because I'm going to write a sample essay as I write this book, here is how I'm starting:

Love

Religion

Science

Human ~~Fre~~ Rights

Personnel   Management

Ecology

War

You'll note that the above list contains the sample Subjects from p. 2. If you wish, you can start working right now on a free choice Subject of your own, and by the time you finish this book, you'll have a completed writing project.

Now, look at the list. Start making some decisions. Which of the general Subjects *really* appeals to you? Are there two or three which for some reason seem more interesting than the others? Decide. Then, cross out the others. Here's what I have done.

Love

~~Religion~~

~~Science~~

~~Human Fire Rights~~

Personnel Management

~~Ecology~~

War

I could, I suppose, write something on Religion, Science, Human Rights, or Ecology, but I don't want to. Why? I'm not really certain. Your reasons for rejecting certain general Subjects will usually vary. How much research would be needed? How much time do you have? How interested are you? How much experience have you had? Who is your audience? These and many other considerations will affect your choice. Believe it or not, so will the weather, the amount of sleep you had the night before, and the compatibility of your marriage. I selected Love, Personnel Management, and War for all the above reasons.

What is important, however, is that you give yourself a choice.

You are now ready to begin the limiting process. Take a new sheet of yellow paper, turn it sideways, write your three Subjects at the top, then create three Topics for each Subject. Remember that your Topics should derive from but be more limited than your Subjects. Your yellow sheet should now look like this:

You can see, perhaps, why I suggested that you turn the page sideways. One of the most important writing habits you should establish is always to use *lots* of paper. Leave spaces and wide margins on your preliminary and draft pages so that you can fill them in later with comments, notes, changes, and specific illustrative details.

Notice that by creating nine Topics from the three Subjects, I have given myself even a greater variety of choice. There is no way, however, that at this stage I can begin to write an essay about anything.

Much more limiting is needed.

Continuing the limiting process, you should now create three Limited Topics for each of your Topics. Here's how:

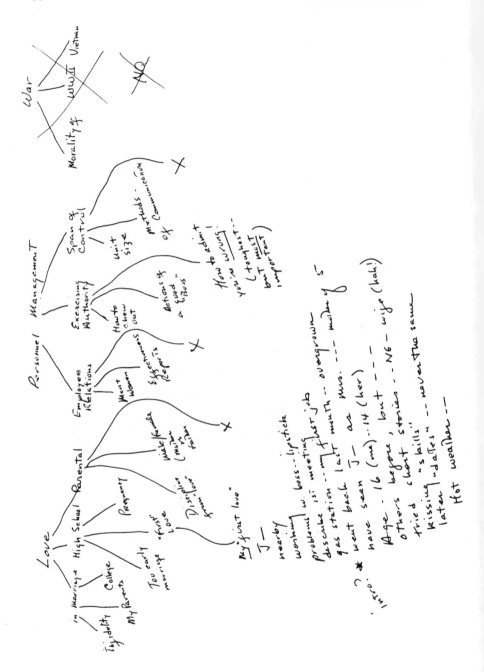

I've been timing myself. To accomplish the previous page took me sixteen minutes, a time period which included one distraction when the telephone rang. The call was for my wife. (If at all possible, get away from a telephone while you're writing. If you cannot, learn not to jump too high when your concentration is abruptly broken.)

In sixteen minutes I created fifteen Limited Topics, each of which has specific potential for an essay. In addition, one of those Limited Topics intrigued me, so I jotted some additional notes.

Look carefully at my Subjects, Topics, and Limited Topics. Can you see how the limiting process works? Under Personnel Management, for instance, the Topic "Exercising Authority" suggested three less general Limited Topics: "How to chew out" ("I'd write on such matters as tone of voice, scolding *only* in private situations, and how to administer oral and written reprimands); "Actions of a Good Boss" (here, I might consider appearance, language, promptness, and loyalty); and "How to admit you're wrong!" (I have substantial experience in this area).

Notice how each Topic not only derives from its antecedent but is much more specific. Regardless of what you write, you can almost never limit too much during the conceiving process, and somewhere in your mass of preliminary notes is the brick you're searching for.

There's nothing mystic, by the way, about my use of *three* Subjects, Topics, and Limited Topics. Obviously, you could work with four or more of each, but I've found that unless I restrict to three, my planning pages get too messy. Three of each seem to work. Two, I think, are too few to give you enough ideas to throw away.

For most writing projects, this process of limiting is always the same: you should start by brainstorming a large number of Subjects, Topics, and Limited Topics, knowing that most of what you are writing down will not be applicable. Why? Without an opportunity to reject unworkable ideas, you may get halfway through an essay on a Topic you selected too soon and then realize that what you're writing is going nowhere. Alas, it's too late, so you wrap the thing up somehow, hand it in, and pray that everyone else had a more severe case of the same disease.

Don't write yourself into this kind of dilemma. Discarding preliminary ideas is easy. Often, it seems as if the choice is being made for you *while* you're creating Limited Topics. For instance, look again at page 14. Note how my three Limited Topics under "Love" (Subject) and "Married Love" (Topic) are quite different from each other. Notice also, however, that under the other Topic of "Parental" love, the Limited Topic of "Male/Female (Mother/Father)" is quite similar to the second Limited Topic, "Parents," and that I have drawn an "X" where a third Limited Topic might go. The similarity of these two Limited Topics and the existence of that "X" tell me that I'm running out of ideas and that I probably don't want to write about this Topic.

The same problem is evident with the Topics "Employee Relations" and "Span of Control," as well as with the entire Subject of "War." By the time I reached the "War" Subject, I was not only getting tired but was also thinking back about that "First Love" Limited Topic, and rather than continue the process of limiting what I did *not* really want to write about, I decided to go back and play with the idea which had suddenly seemed to interest me. I wrote the notes under "My 'First Love' " *after* I had crossed out the Subject of "War."

This same experience has happened to most of my writing students, and it will happen to you. By using this method of arriving at a Limited Topic, you'll actually be preventing the "Blank Page Syndrome" by creating all those irrelevant notes (irrelevant for the moment, that is. Actually, you may have done some preliminary sketching for your next few writing projects. Don't throw anything away).

Buried in this always disparate list should be a Limited Topic which will interest you and about which you can write. Practice this process. Try limiting your own Subjects from pages 2 and 3.

Assigned Topics

I mentioned earlier that the process of conceiving an assigned writing project is the same as that for a "free" one. Here's what I meant. If you have been given what you're certain is a detailed, specific assignment such as "Methods of Diminishing Erosion in Colorado Eastern Slope Cornfields," go through exactly the same limiting exercise as I have just discussed, but realize that you may be entering the process in the middle. As with a "free" Subject, you'll want to create Topics and Limited Topics which you can discard. In this case, move *up* the abstraction ladder and create a Topic, "Farm Erosion," and a Subject, "Farming." Then see if you can devise additional Limited Topics which parallel the one which you have been assigned. Here is how such an exercise might look.

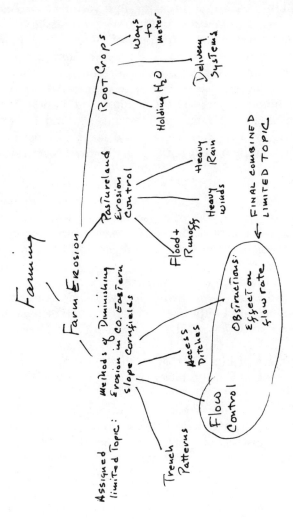

Notice what has happened. I began by writing down the assignment as a Limited Topic under the Topic (which I created, working backwards) of "Farm Erosion." Then I invented two other Limited Topics that were roughly parallel to the assignment: "Pasturelands" and "Root Crop" erosion control. Then I began limiting each one, breaking into various components the process of irrigation itself until, under my assigned Topic, I arrived at a further Limited Topic of "Flow Control" methods. You can see the circles. Depending upon the time available (and if I had the engineering knowledge, of course), I could write a satisfactorily limited paper, complete with charts and diagrams, on the Limited Topic, "The Cheapest and Easiest Method of Regulating Natural Irrigation Flow in Colorado Eastern Slope Cornfields." By briefly discussing the more expensive methods and dismissing them early in the paper, I could cover the assigned ground.

Actually, I would probably limit even further, as one of my students recently did. A bright Civil Engineering major who feared writing and saw little use for it in his "real" world of computers and matrixes, this student was having difficulty selecting something to write about. We talked, and from my questions which forced him to go through a verbal limiting process very similar to the written one, his interest in irrigation became obvious. I played a role: "I'm Farmer Jones," I said, "And every time I open my headgate I either get too damn much or too damn little water." The student smiled and asked me if I knew about the "_____" (a technical term which I have, unfortunately, forgotten). I told him no, that my daddy had taught me everything I knew and that I'd never been to that fancy University up the river.

The student began sketching, and within five minutes had shown me a diagram of a flow-regulating system that used specifically shaped obstructions placed in the access and primary irrigation ditches. Ironically, the obstructions looked just like some of Pirsig's bricks. "All right," I said. "There's your paper. Assume that your audience is a group of well-intentioned but non-technical farmers. Show them how to regulate their water irrigation intake."

He seemed bewildered, this engineering student who was about to learn what selecting a Limited Topic was all about. "You mean I can write on something I like?" he asked.

"What else is there," I replied, and I believe it still. You *can* write on something you like—if you'll give yourself the chance to find it. If you can learn how to conceive a properly Limited Topic *before* you actually start stringing sentences together, you will invariably end up writing about something which not only interests you but which has intellectual or practical significance as well. LIMIT. LIMIT. LIMIT. You'll find that brick, even if your discovery seems accidental.

One final note—about love. I usually try to dissuade my students from writing on such emotional abstractions as Love, Hate, Fear, or Beauty, simply because inexperienced writers find it difficult to achieve the distance and objectivity which are required to produce a good paper. I think you should avoid even such limited topics as "The Sweetest Sister Anyone Can Have" or "My Mom"—unless you can look at yourself ironically[3] and with a cold, fishy eye.

Having made this pronouncement, I'll now get back to work on a sample essay for the next few chapters of this book. It's going to be on the Limited Topic I arrived at earlier: "My First Love." Perhaps by now I can achieve the required objectivity, and anyway, I've been wanting to write about this Topic for years.

---

[3]Another dictionary exercise. "Ironic" does *not* mean "satiric" or "sardonic."

Chapter 3

Thesis and Audience

THIS CHAPTER WILL BE SHORT. The topic, however, is important. Without a sense of your audience and without a strong Thesis, usually expressed by a Thesis Statement which you should write down before starting your rough draft, your writing project cannot be as good as it should be. Without a Thesis created with a specific audience in mind, your final essay will probably be boring, mushy, incoherent, and confused, and if you are blessed with one of the few good instructors or supervisors, all that will happen to you is that you'll be asked to rewrite the paper or report. Most of the time, however, you'll either receive another sad C–, or your project will simply disappear somewhere and you'll hear nothing more about it—until you ask your boss why you didn't receive a raise.

Audience

If you aren't certain who your audience is, imagine one—
always. Keep your audience in mind throughout the writing

process. For instance, although I have no idea *who* you are, I do know something about you. You are reading this book because you (1) think you need to improve your writing; (2) lack the confidence that *everything* you write will turn out satisfactorily; (3) are interested in picking up some writing tips from a professional who has managed (often because of pure luck) to publish quite a few words; and (4) did not want to buy one of those "other" writing books which are so imposing, complex, and expensive. Of course you may have been *assigned* this book; regardless, the four reasons should still apply. If they do not, I suggest that you change jobs or drop the course in which you're enrolled. Don't continue to waste your and others' time.

With you as audience in mind, I know that I am *not* creating *Writing From Scratch* for readers who want to learn fine points of grammar, syntax, style, or language. The books listed in the Appendix, especially Strunk and White's *Elements of Style,* will provide more specific information. Throughout *Writing From Scratch* I will be addressing the not yet self-confident writer (that's *you*) who should realize that those who cannot communicate well invariably end up working for those who *can,* and who also recognizes the extreme need for effective, precise communication in the modern world. The triumph of technology does not replace the need to communicate; rather, technology increases that need. An example happened one day to an acquaintance of mine, a pilot who was flying a large military aircraft. Noticing that his final approach to the runway was too low, he barked the order to his co-pilot, "Takeoff Power." He meant that the throttles should be moved full forward, as for takeoff. His co-pilot "took off" power—by pulling the throttles to idle. The result? One very bent aircraft and two embarrassed young men. One misunderstood word had caused a major accident. No one, fortunately, was hurt.

All communication, whether written or oral, must be directed *toward* someone, and when writing anything, you must always know your audience. If you are writing a paper on improving Employee Effectiveness Reports, for instance, do you plan to address Management? The Supervisors? The Employees? Students in a Business Course? Each audience has different levels of interest, experience, and language skills, and a paper which delights one group might bore another. If you are writing literary criticism, for example, consider your readers. A *review* assumes that its audience has *not* read the book being reviewed, but a critical essay should be directed toward readers who are intimately, often professionally acquainted with the novel, poem, or play under discussion. Those of us who profess literature scream often in the sanctity of our offices when we read yet another student's plot summary of a novel. When you write an essay or an examination question in an English class, *never* summarize the plot. Talk *about* the plot. You don't have to show the instructor that you've read the book. If you haven't, that fact will become obvious in the first paragraph. Give your audience the respect it deserves.

The need to keep your audience in mind applies to any writing that you ever do. That paper on Erosion Control, for example, would use completely different language and examples if written for "Farmer John" instead of for an International Crop Erosion Symposium. So would my planned essay on "First Love" have different form and content if I wrote it for young teenagers and not for their parents. (I really dislike that word, "teenager." So did all of my children when they were in their pre-twenties years. Like so many words, however, "teenage" is about the best categorical word we have.) A younger group might be looking forward to a first "love"; the parents would be looking *back*. Or what about directing this same essay to a University class in Adolescent Behavior? In this instance, I would no doubt be expected to use psychological jargon such as "post-pubescent stress syndrome" or "adult role-model intensification." Ironically, because I refuse to use such jargon, my paper might not be well received by certain professional groups who prefer to write in languages which barely resemble English.

Selecting and keeping your audience in mind determine not only the language that you will use but also the assumptions behind and the intent of your paper, the points you will make, the examples you will use, and your essay's overall tone. I once began a conversation with a group of foreign pilots who had been speaking what I thought was Hebrew by mentioning how impressed I was with the Israeli Air Force. After quite an icy silence, one of the pilots informed me in English that they were from Saudi Arabia. If you make equally wrong audience assessments, you too will block communication, especially on such subjects as birth control, abortion, conservative economic policy, the Cold War, the Equal Rights Amendment, or women's rights. *Always keep your audience in mind.*

Thesis and Thesis Statement

Equally important (and usually keyed directly toward that specific audience) is the Thesis of your project. The Thesis of an essay is the major proposition on which your entire work is based. Although you may certainly present opinions and evidence for an opposing view, your essay should primarily define, develop, and document *one* major thesis. It does not matter how long or how complex the project is—you should *always* have a single thesis in mind before and during the actual writing process. For *Writing From Scratch,* my thesis is as follows:

> The basic principles of good writing can best be shown in a short book by actually writing an essay, and as the general methods and techniques of writing are discussed, the essay itself will be written.

Except for this example, my thesis appears nowhere in this book. It is, however, the overriding proposition which governs *Writing From Scratch.* Usually arrived at before the organizational process is complete, the Thesis of a project is often refined and changed during the structuring stages. If you begin, for instance, with the thesis that "People Are No Damned Good," and then because of reflection, research, and more experience decide that there are a few nice people around after all, you might decide to revise your thesis to read, "People Over Thirty Are No Damned Good." Note that this change also exemplifies the never-ending limiting process. I wouldn't advise such a thesis, incidentally, for as Mr. Jerry Rubin (who coined the 1960's phrase "never trust anyone over thirty") discovered, we all eventually reach that age and thus become equally untrustworthy.

What do you do with your Thesis once you have created it? Write it down on a separate single sheet of paper (you may use white paper here when you are certain that your thesis will not change) and tack or tape it wherever you cannot help looking at it while you write. Mine is pinned on my corkboard beside a copy of the preliminary Table of Contents for *Writing From Scratch*.

Once again, you do *not* have to quote your Thesis in your essay—but you must write one for your own use. Constant visual reference to your written thesis will keep you from digressing or writing yourself up one of those many blind alleys into which most writers too often wander.

Usually, you will find a further refinement of your original Thesis is needed. Many teachers of writing suggest that you create a Thesis Statement. In most of my own writing, especially in shorter (500–4000 words) articles or reports, I find such a Thesis Statement necessary.

A Thesis Statement adds to and develops *cause* for the Thesis and helps you organize your essay. "Some People Are No Damned Good *because* they lie, cheat, and steal." "The Best Place to Reprimand Employees is in Private *because* doing so allows the employee to respond without embarrassment, assures the employee's anonymity, and protects the Boss in case there has been an error." "One can never forget one's first 'Love', *because* . . ." *Because* . . . . I'm not ready yet. Soon, perhaps. Maybe it's a bad Topic after all.

You should notice some commonalities in the above examples. First, each Thesis Statement contains the word "because." Always writing this word in your Thesis Statement forces you to finish the sentence, in effect requiring you to develop your thesis before you start writing about it. Completing a "because" sentence often causes a modification of your original thesis. "People Are No Damned Good," for instance, "because they lie, cheat, and steal" sounds sardonically brash and can be easily argued by those who are honest. Adding "Some" to the Thesis, however, makes it more justifiable.

A second commonality in these sample Thesis Statements is that the rule of three seems to have reappeared (remember the Topic Limiting exercise?). Most of the short to medium sized writing projects you attempt can be handled by creating a Thesis Statement which is supported by three major points after the "because." As I'll show in Chapter 4, even if you begin with more than three major points in mind, you can usually resolve them into three major points to develop and discuss.

Finally, you should understand that after the word "because," each of these Thesis Statements (regardless of their essential validity) contains three points that are roughly balanced in significance and size. I mean *size*. Here is a revision which violates this balance: "Some People Are No Damned Good because they lie, cheat, and my little brother stole my watch." Although this example is obviously strained, it represents one of the major structural flaws which inexperienced writers build into their essays. After you write the first version of your next Thesis Statement, examine it carefully to make certain that the phrases following the word "because" are balanced. One cannot imagine the "evil" of one's little brother's theft as being equivalent to all the lying and cheating that goes on in this world.

You can see, I think, how closely linked are the requirements of Thesis and Audience. For a particular religious denomination, your Thesis on Birth Control might differ entirely from one which you would present to a scientific group. Even if you decided to challenge the beliefs of your audience, you should still adapt your Thesis to make certain that the audience would at least listen to your own views. Had I amended my opening statement to those Saudi Arabians, perhaps saying only that I was pleased that they, too, were undergoing training in the United States, I probably would have achieved *some* communication, at least.

Remember *Audience* and *Thesis*—always.

Chapter 4

Structuring

WHEN YOU WERE A CHILD, you no doubt built a number of highly satisfactory, unusual, stable structures out of wood blocks. Tinkertoy sections, or even toothpicks—all without any plan in mind. These structures certainly served their immediate purposes, but they were not designed to last. Furthermore—and most important—each of their components had been pre-cut or shaped, and whatever excellence you achieved was only partly a result of your ingenuity. Actually, your structure remained standing until you took it apart because you were working with materials which were already designed to balance each other and to fit.

The act of constructing a writing project is similar to putting building blocks together, with two important differences: first, writing *is* designed to last; and second, you, the architect, must also create and shape each block. If you structure your essay properly *before, during,* and *after* (I mean *after*—see Chapter 7) the writing of your rough draft, you will produce a finished product that will stand by itself, forever. Such a piece of writing can be challenged, certainly, but it cannot be condemned. One indication of an essay's excellence, I think, appears when a reader says, "I disagree with everything you say," then presents his or her views. In effect, this reader is saying "I don't like the ideas which are *so well presented* that I want to take issue with them." When this reaction occurs, you know that you've written well. Your reader is saying that *you* are wrong, not that your *paper* is wrong.

Scratch Outlines

To achieve satisfactory structure in an essay, you should again realize that no piece of writing springs perfectly from the human imagination. As an example, here again are my jottings under the Subject, "Love":

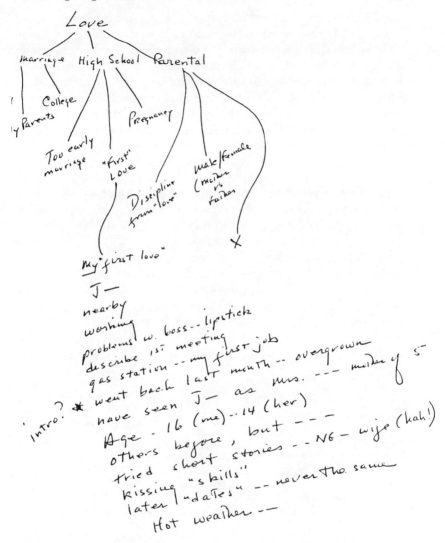

What these disparate, random comments constitute are some of the building blocks for an essay—but there is obviously no balance or even recognizable shape to any of them.

Allowing my thoughts on this first Limited Topic to wander freely, I created this list in just a few moments. J— refers to the girl's name; "nearby" indicates where she lived; "working" is further refined by the phrase "Gas station—my first job." I had not thought about the situation or the person for years until I drove by a former home a few weeks ago—hence the entry "went back last month—overgrown." The rest of the words and phrases all derive from and have relevance to the Limited Topic—*but not necessarily to each other.* Before starting to write a rough draft, I must do more work. I know from experience that much (sometimes most) of my original thoughts about an intriguing Limited Topic will eventually be discarded or at least substantially altered.

To begin the structuring process, you should create such a Scratch Outline—usually nothing more than a list of ideas which in some way illustrate your Limited Topic. If you have a Thesis in mind, fine; if you don't, let the outlining process help you create one. Start by looking over your list. (I have been staring at mine, wondering how I got myself into this mess.) Search for relationships, similarities, differences. For instance, I can see that the phrases "went back last month," "Have seen J— as Mrs. — mother of 5," and "tried short stories—NG" are related because they all describe events which happened *after* the experience. Also, "my first job" and "Age 16 (me)—14 (her)" indicate my experience and age level.

While looking for some kind of associations and annotating my Scratch Outline, I have been writing notes toward a Thesis. Here they are:

Thesis --
Impossible to forget one's first love because:
① Memories will always trigger (SS - Return)
② Significant adult emotional experience
③ Colors (flavors?) future relations?
First Reality v. Illusion

At this stage, I can write a tentative working Thesis: "One can never forget one's first 'love' because somehow, the memories will always be triggered, such an experience is an individual's first contact with 'adult' emotions, and one's future sexual attitudes often derive from this experience."

Of the three parts to this working Thesis, point #1, the triggering of memories, resulted from my having combined three of the comments I had circled as ① on my Scratch Outline. Here's the revised outline:

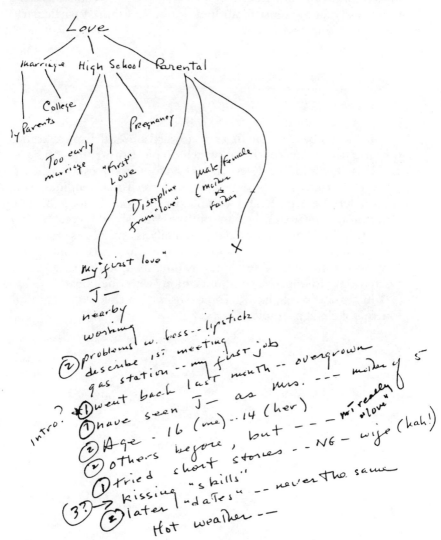

Thesis point #2, 'adult' emotions, seem to fit the items I've circled as ②, and point #3, future relations, may be vaguely connected to the phrase "kissing skills." Please note the question mark after the number ③. I'm not at all comfortable with this part of my tentative Thesis. I now have this Thesis Statement tacked on my bulletin board. It's a start—but only a start, I fear. I don't really have a sense of audience; nor do I think I particularly want to try and prove point #3.

Topic Outlines

I do have, however, the first step toward a useful Topic Outline, the structuring device without which no piece of writing can be as good as it could be. Even though many good essays can be produced from quickly developed, sparse Topic Outlines, you should let the length and complexity of your writing project determine how extensive an outline you should create. You cannot, for instance, write a detailed analysis of a 20-year national political trend from a short Topic Outline; but you certainly don't have to create an outline nearly as long as a 500-word essay to discuss ways to improve communications with one's boss.

You must, though, have a Topic Outline which looks something like this skeletal example:

THESIS STATEMENT: "_____ because
1. _____, 2. _____, 3. _____."

TOPIC OUTLINE:
[Introduction]

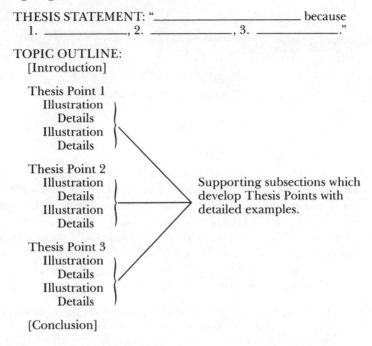

Thesis Point 1
  Illustration
    Details
  Illustration
    Details

Thesis Point 2
  Illustration
    Details
  Illustration
    Details

Thesis Point 3
  Illustration
    Details
  Illustration
    Details

Supporting subsections which develop Thesis Points with detailed examples.

[Conclusion]

Only when your completed outline resembles this example are you ready to start writing the text of your essay. Looking at the initial working thesis of my "Love" Topic, I can see some problems to solve before I can achieve the kind of balance I need. Also, I still have not determined the audience toward which I want to direct my essay.

Organizing Principles

It is usually at this point in the writing process that the undisciplined writer fails to take the few extra minutes necessary to create a good structure for a project. What you should do now is pause and think, not about *what* you want to say but instead about *how* you want to say it. By now you should have some idea of thesis and of the illustrations you will use; now you should decide which of the basic organizational principles you want to use.

There are five basic organizing principles:

SPATIAL

TEMPORAL

CAUSE to EFFECT

COMPARISON AND CONTRAST

ASCENDING IMPORTANCE

One of these principles, often used in conjunction with one or more of the others, will provide a structure for almost anything you will be asked to write.

SPATIAL organization best orders Limited Topics such as a description of a certain steel plant, a narration of a difficult ascent up a mountain peak, or a discussion of a new dress design. Whenever the description of some thing or visually developed action is the main intention of your project, let Spatial ("happening or existing in space") organization be your primary mode. Here's an example for a paper on the Limited Topic, "An Average High School Student's Room":

THESIS STATEMENT: The neat outward appearance of an average high school student's room is as deceptive as the tip of an iceberg, *because* most of the surprises lie hidden in drawers, under the bed, and in the closet.

OUTLINE:
[Introduction]

Thesis Point #1: Drawers
Illustration: Dresser to left of door
Illustration: Small Chest beside bed

Thesis Point#2: The Bed—What lies under the dust ruffle
Illustration: Hard Objects (boxes, shoes, etc.)
Illustration: Soft objects (clothes, crumpled paper)

Thesis Point #3: The Closet, or, The Warehouse
Illustration: Objects over 4' tall (bicycle, skiis)
Illustration: Objects under 4' tall (suitcases, backpack, etc.)

[Conclusion]

When spatially describing such a room, you should guide the reader's eye in a regular progression, perhaps from left to right, without making the reader's eye jump haphazardly from place to place and back again. Proper Spatial organization is as regular as a correct head-to-toe description of a human figure: you would not start by describing a person's hair, then mention shoes, then shirt, then hat. In essence, a spatially organized essay forces a reader to see the logical progression from one point in space to another.

TEMPORAL organization is similar to Spatial, but here, *time* governs. Appropriate Limited Topics which can be presented temporally are a child's maturing in grade school, an analysis of a die-making process, or the strategy of winning a 10-kilometer closed course bicycle race. As with Spatial organization, you should be particularly careful *not* to disrupt the time sequence from beginning to end. Here again is the Limited Topic about a student's room, but with a new Thesis and Temporal organization:

> THESIS STATEMENT: My High School son's pattern of conceal-ment is regular *because* he first stuffs his dresser and chest drawers, then fills every nook and cranny under his bed, then stashes what's left over in his closet.
>
> OUTLINE:
> [Introduction]
>
> Thesis Point #1: Drawers
> Illustration: Most easily accessible
> Illustration: First hiding place he comes to
>
> Thesis Point #2: Under Bed
> Illustration:
> Illustration:
>
> Thesis Point #3: In Closet
> Illustration: Used only when others are filled up
> Illustration: Least accessible
>
> [Conclusion]

I'd like you to notice something about the above outline. I had difficulty creating satisfactory illustrations for Thesis Point #2, even though the temporal idea seemed workable at first. When you experience this problem on a project of yours, STOP. Try another method of organization. As happened here, an organiz-ing principle you attempt to use may not fit your idea—so discard it. For an essay on my son's room, I would probably find Spatial organization to be the best.

The next organizational principle, CAUSE AND EFFECT, usually best fits writing projects which answer the question "Why?" *Why* were Vietnam veterans so poorly received when they came home? *Why* is a perpetual motion machine impossible to build? *Why* can't I get that young lady (she didn't seem so young at the time) out of my mind? Just a minute. I've been jotting again:

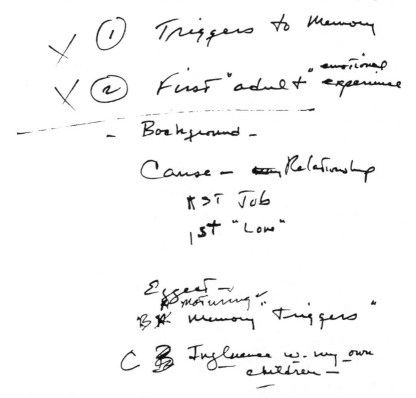

Thinking of Cause and Effect organization made me consider my essay again. Here's a possible way to write it. Notice how my thesis has changed:

THESIS: One's first "love" can and should not be forgotten because of the effect it has on one's maturing process, events keep triggering memories, and these memories help one understand what one's own children are going through.

I now have a new thesis statement ready for the corkboard. Let's see how it works in a Cause to Effect Outline:

[INTRO -]

Cause: The Relationship -
    1st Job - gas station
    Job description -- living nearby
    1st meeting
    Dating..
    Development of Relationship
    Incidents [don't tell all]
    Later dating
    Breakup -- [can remember?]

Effect:
    Maturing -
      Emotional
      Sexual [maybe not]
      Being above board + honest

    Relation Past to remember --
      Triggers -
      Description of events

Understanding Own children's
      [similar incidents - select
        ones which would have
        caused us most grief.

[Conclusion -]

Compare my new thesis with my first one on page 30. This change exemplifies what I said earlier about one's Thesis often developing *during* the structuring process. My new Thesis also illustrates why I put those arrows joining Thesis Statement and Outline on the Basic Law. This essay may work after all. Audience? How about writing for parents of children who are just showing those first unmistakable signs of being in "love"? Perhaps. More later.

The fourth organizational principle is that of COMPARISON AND CONTRAST. This one can be used whenever you are showing how a new process differs from an older one, when you are writing about your company's sales record being better or worse than that of a competitor's, or whenever you wish to show that something is either *like* or *unlike* something else. For young people, today's "first love" is different from yesterday's *because*. . . . No, I don't want to write my essay this way.

When comparing or contrasting, remember this distinction: you should compare like objects, using the phrase "compare *with*"; you should contrast *un*like objects, using the words "in contrast *to*."

Here is another outline for the teenager's room Limited Topic, organized by using both Comparison and Contrast:

THESIS STATEMENT: Although my two children's rooms appear similar, my son's room has more surprises because of what he puts in his dresser and chest drawers, his under-the-bed treasure trove, and his closet warehouse.

OUTLINE:
[Introduction]
    COMPARISON: Son's and daughter's rooms (external view)
                  Dresser and Chest
                  Bed
                  Closet
    CONTRAST: (under the surface lies the truth)

Thesis Point #1: Drawers
                Daughter's
                Son's

Thesis Point #2: Under Bed
                Daughter's
                Son's

Thesis Point #3: Closet
                Daughter's
                Son's
[Conclusion]

Anyone who has both sons and daughters knows that this Limited Topic could be argued either way. Regardless, the success of an essay on this subject would result from the way it is structured and then illustrated with pertinent details.

Whether you decide to use either Comparison, Contrast, or a combination of the two often depends upon the entries you make on your Topic limiting exercise. What you decide at first *not* to write about may actually provide a good contrast to your final choice. Look at page 14 again. Under the subject of "Management," Topic of "Exercising Authority," Limited Topic of "How to admit you're wrong," I could write an effective essay by contrasting the "good" boss to a "bad" one, that supervisor who might not be able to communicate and who might spend too much time chewing out subordinates instead of admitting culpability.[1] These substantive ideas for a potential contrast came from the notes I jotted down for *other* Limited Topics. See them? Always keep your foul matter close to you while writing, and use it. Many times, ideas which you think you've discarded can be put to good use later.

The final organizational principle that you should consider for any essay is that of ASCENDING IMPORTANCE—and I have saved this method until last because it is probably the most important one you should know. Discussing Ascending Importance at this point exemplifies the process itself. Put simply, the principle of Ascending Importance requires that you save your biggest gun for last. Never write an essay which resembles a late-night joke telling session, when all the good jokes are told early, and by the end, only the dregs remain. You can organize almost any essay by Ascending Importance; to do so you should evaluate your points after you list them on your Scratch Outline, then determine a rank order of importance, and finally, identify that order by letters or numbers on the Scratch Outline.

For instance, here is an example of the Ascending Order principle applied to the Limited Topic, "Actions of a good Boss." Note the changes which took place as I developed the idea.

[1] I haven't forgotten the 65% of you who should look this word up.

~~Characteristics~~
~~Actions~~ of a "good" Boss

① promptness
① appearance
③ honesty
③ reliability
① ~~③~~ Thoughtfulness

① knowing employees personally
② listening
③ being consistent
② knowing what everyone does
① ~~③~~ delegating authority
② being available
① entertaining
③ → keeping word
② backing up employees

~~Thesis~~   ① External actions

② Personal ~~Thoughts~~ Interest

③ Basic ~~Beliefs~~ Commitment

Thesis: A good "Boss" can be
recognized because of his or
her ~~external~~ actions toward
employees, personal interest
in Their as human beings, and ~~&~~
~~of the~~ basic ~~commitment to~~ humanity.
~~The job~~

Examine this Scratch Outline carefully. I created a working Thesis by listing as many characteristics as I could; then, looking for relationships and associations, I grouped these characteristics into the three subtopics written below the list. As I decided upon these subtopics, I consciously ranked them in order of importance:

External Actions [necessary]

Personal Interest [more important]

Basic Committment [invaluable]

This time, the three divisions just *happened* to fall into what I consider to be the order of ascending importance (without a basic committment to human values, no supervisor can succeed, regardless of his or her external actions). After confirming this order, I wrote the numbers beside the appropriate words and phrases on the list.

At this point, however, I was not certain what the proper order within each subsection should be, so I recopied the general characteristics, then determined the internal order of the details. Here is this stage in the structuring process:

[Introduction]

(Audience: employees who will
          be future bosses) .

   I. External Actions

     ② promptness
     ① appearance
     ③ Thoughtfulness
     ④ knowing employees personally
     (delegating authority) → Intro ?
     ({entertaining} ?)

   II. Personal Interest

     ④⑤ listening
     2 ② knowing what employees do
     3 ③ availability
     5 ④ backing up employees

   III. Basic Commitment

     ③ honesty
     ② reliability -- keeping word
     ① consistency

[concl]

Of particular interest is my disposition of the two characteristics "delegating authority" and "entertaining." They just didn't seem to fit, so I made a note perhaps to consider mentioning them in an introduction. Also, notice my parenthetical comment on Audience. I suspect that my decision to direct the paper to employees helped me determine what order I would use.

Finally, here is an example of a Topic Outline for this same Limited Topic. Note that not only is the overall outline organized according to the principle of Ascending Importance, but so is each subsection. Note also that I have added a third element: more specific illustrations, the essence of a paper which gives it the salty crispness I mentioned earlier.

THESIS STATEMENT: Employees can always recognize a good "Boss" because of that supervisor's external actions, personal interest in them, and overall basic humanity.

TOPIC OUTLINE:
[Introduction]

    I. External Actions
       A. Appearance
          1. Clothing
          2. Decisiveness
       B. Promptness
          1. In own office
          2. For appointments
       C. Thoughtfulness
          1. Toward employees on job
          2. Personal attitudes off-job
            (Use as transition to II)

    II. Personal Interest (trans from before)
       A. Knowing employees personally
          1. Past record
          2. Personal profiles—like/dislikes/hobbies
       B. Knowledge of employees' jobs
          1. General work area
          2. Specific tasks
       C. Avilability to employees
          1. In office
          2. After duty hours
       D. Listening to employees
          1. Gripes
          2. New ideas
       ~~E. Standing behind employees~~

move to III B 2 ↳→

   III. Basic Humanity
      A. Consistency
         1. Attitude toward company
         2. Not changing mind on issues
      B. Reliability
         1. Keeping one's cool
         2. Backing up employees when they're right
      C. Honesty
         1. Can be believed at all times
         2. No double dealing

[Conclusion]

As I was typing this sample outline, I decided that the subsection "Standing behind Employees" did not fit under II—so I moved it to III, B, 2. The adapting process *never* stops.

This sample outline would provide the structure for a 1000-word (about four typewritten pages) essay or report. What would determine its length would be the number of specific examples used to develop each illustration. I'm certain that you can remember a time when your supervisor or professor showed up late without an excuse—and the time that same person refused to accept your reasons for tardiness. There's a specific example which would fit well as an example for I, B, 2 (above).

For every one of your writing projects, you should consider at least one of these five organizing principles—and you should always follow these three steps:

First: Brainstorm the Limited Topic and write a Scratch Outline.

Second: Play with the Scratch Outline and decide upon a *Main* organizing principle (Spatial, Temporal, Cause to Effect, Comparison and Contrast, Ascending Importance).

Third: Create a Topic Outline.

I have watched my students use this process in class, and after some practice, many of them can create a good Topic Outline for either a free or assigned Subject in as short a time as ten minutes. So can you.

Some Final Aspects of Structuring

Regardless of which organizing principle you select as primary for your project, you can use the others as well. When you create a Topic Outline, know not only what your *overall* structural plan is but also what the plan for each of your internal divisions should be. In the case of the "Boss" essay, I organized each subsection by Ascending Importance, but I could have illustrated each A, B, and C by using Cause to Effect. For instance, by using specific examples of lateness or forgetfulness (Cause), I could show how a supervisor can offend employees (Effect). You should try to follow a regular pattern of principles, no matter which one(s) you use. Most important, always know what you're doing, and why.

Also, before you write the rough draft you should examine your outline to make certain that it conforms to three basic structural requirements:

BALANCE

EQUAL RANK

POINTBACK

Remember what I said earlier about Thesis—that each sentence of your Thesis should consider something of approximately the same *size?* The same principle applies to your outline. If your Thesis is balanced, so will be your major headings (I, II, III). Your subsections, too, should be similarly balanced. Here's an example of *improper* balance, based on the "Boss" outline:

I. External Actions

    A. Appearance
       1. Clothing
       2. Decisiveness
       3. Tone of voice
       4. Cheerfulness
       5. Neatness of office

    B. Promptness
       1. On time for work

    C. Thoughtfulness
       1. Toward employees on job
          a. Gifts for secretaries
          b. Greeting in morning
          c. Remembering birthdays
          d. Complimenting for good job

Many of my Topic Outlines have looked just like this one—at an early stage of their development. You can see the lack of balance. If you try to write from such an outline, the problem is obvious: your essay will be just as unbalanced as your outline. Recognize this fault when you commit it—and fix it before you start writing. Here's one way to solve the previous problem:

I. External Actions

    A. Appearance on the job
       1. Clothing
       2. Decisive tone of voice at all times
       3. Neat working conditions
       4. Punctuality—always

    B. Thoughtfulness toward employees
       1. Personal attention and kindnesses
       2. Greetings and use of names
       3. Complimenting good performance

Although not *perfectly* balanced (who among us can be consistently impeccable?), this revised outline would insure a much better essay.

You should also make certain that each of your I's, A's, and subsequent subsections is of "equal rank." Call the I's Generals, if you wish, then the A's become Colonels, the 1's Majors, and so on. In the poorly balanced example (above), "B. Promptness, (etc.)" does not rank equally with the similarly designated other headings of Thoughtfulness and Appearance, so I demoted it to its appropriate rank in revision. You can expect to create many ill-ranked elements in future working outlines—but you should recognize faults and correct them. As I did with my note on "Delegating Authority," if you can't make all parts of your outline fit, throw the offending entries out. Your essay will be the better for it.

Finally, each element of your outline must Point Back to its superior—and all elements must Point Back to your Thesis. Diagrammed, the Point Back requirement looks like this:

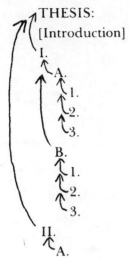

THESIS:

[Introduction]

I.

   A.

     1.

     2.

     3.

   B.

     1.

     2.

     3.

II.

   A.

(the same principle applies throughout)

Make certain while creating, but especially when you are evaluating your Topic Outline that each subordinate section does in fact develop and illustrate the idea stated by its heading. If an entry is unbalanced or unequal, move it somewhere else—or again, just throw it out. Merely because something is a good and true idea does not mean that it belongs in any particular essay—even if you, the god-author, gave birth to it.

Adherence to these three principles, Balance, Equal Rank, and Point Back, will assure you of creating a structural plan that will lead to a good piece of writing.

How to apply all this theory to my *own* project? I'll stop writing this book and go back to my Thesis and rough outline.

*   *   *

Time: 42 minutes later.

So far, I've spent about an hour on this essay.

With my revised Thesis Statement and Scratch Outline from pages 30–31 in front of me, I began trying to create a refined, balanced Thesis Statement which would develop an essay in a Cause to Effect mode. Here is my first attempt:

Thesis
Statement:

~~It is~~
~~One's~~

Remembering (the exact details of and reaction to) one's first "love" is important because ① you can't block it out because of the constant reminders, ② as a part of your maturing process, it affected your present attitudes, and ③ it helps you understand (to a certain extent anyway) your own children.

[Intro] ← the trip (describe now -- overgrown)

② ⟨?⟩ I   The Relationship (cause)

II   The Aftermath (effect)

A. 3. Maturing
A. B. Triggers

C. Own children

I and II were to create the basic Cause and Effect structure, with IIA, IIB, and IIC to be organized Temporally. I realized, however, that I could also incorporate the principle of Ascending Importance, but as I evaluated this possibility, I saw flaws. This outline was not following my Thesis Statement, and you can see my lack of confidence in the positioning of IIA and IIB. Finally, no matter how I tried, I could not envision how this outline would fit into a desired three-part division.

It occurred to me that this kind of personal essay often fits well into *any* mode of organization, so I decided to see if I could use three principles at once: Cause to Effect, Ascending Importance, *and* Temporal. Here is how I began to reshape:

Asc. Imp	Cause + Effect	Temporal
I. The Relationship	(cause)	then
II. TRIGGERS	(effect)	Afterward
III. Values	(final effect)	Now

Thesis?

① One of the vital experiences in your maturing process

② Always with you -- reminders --

③ Influences your approach to your spouse and children (bad or good) -- they are not you -- but their emotions are similar

Then I wrote another Thesis Statement:

Revised (final?) Thesis: One should remember the events and circumstances of one's first "love" because ① The relationship is one of the most significant aspects of the maturing process, ② more than with other experiences the memory stays with you and is jogged all your life, and ③ many of your attitudes toward spouse and children are determined by how well you understand your adolescent behaviour.

Fortunately, my instinct and memory of past failures caused me to put that question mark after the word "final." The Topic Outline I tried to create turned out to be a disaster. Here it is:

Topic Outline:

[Intro]

I   The Maturing Process

A. The Relationship

B. The Reactions

Boss

Parents

II   The Memories

A. Triggers -- real
① Air base -- stories
② Job -- husband
③ Death --

B. Imagined (the what if's)

III Attitudes determined

A. Spouse (assuming you
married someone else)

B. Children

[concl]

How deceiving appearances can be! On this outline, I, II, and
III are balanced, of equal rank, and point back to the Thesis, but
look at my A's and B's. Compare all the A's: Relationship, Triggers, Spouse. Now compare the B's: Reactions, Imagined (the

what-ifs?), Children. How can one imagine memories, anyway? Although each of the subsections seems to develop its major point, none seems to have a real relationship to the others. What I see here are elements of three possible projects—not an outline for one unified essay.

One bright point: you should notice that I was working toward specifics, at least. Look at IIA. You can never start too soon to jot down elements of specific details.

Try again, I thought. Back to Thesis. LIMIT. LIMIT. LIMIT.

(New) Thesis:

unrequited *
~~unsuccessful~~

One's first ~~experience~~ with "love" ~~never really ends~~ because of its importance in the maturing ~~process~~, its constantly triggered memories, and ~~its~~ function as a standard for ~~your~~ what you thought was introduced you to ~~the~~ adult world.

It ~~was the most~~ -so dominated- was the first experience that obsessed you, ~~it formed your sexual attitudes~~ caused you to become aware of your own vulnerability, and ~~because~~ you can never forget it, it provides a touchstone for eventual maturity.

* I'm thinking of you and your dictionary, even now.

It was during the tortured writing of this revised Thesis State-ment that I may have tripped over my brick. One's first love is indeed a specific experience, but to write about *all* of that experi-ence would be no less difficult than writing a five-hundred-word essay about the United States. When I added the word "unrequited," however, I not only further limited the Topic of my planned essay, but I also determined my audience as well. I'll write for those of you who are presently experiencing or can never forget your first adolescent heartbreak. If you are one of those few people who have never failed in love, you might possibly want to read about the rest of us.

Here's what I wrote next:

Thesis Statement:

One's first unrequited "love affair" is important to understand because it ① represents one's first obsession with another human being, ② it causes one for the first time to experience the feeling of utter, abject, dismal failure, ③ and (because the memory is always alive), it provides a touchstone for eventual maturity.

Topic Outline:

[Intro] - trip back with my wife -- everything overgrown

I   The Obsession

    A   Events
       1. 1st job -- describe
       2. 1st meeting -- describe
       3. Development of Relationship
          (Kind of relationship
            what + where
            "going steady" — later

B. Reaction —

    1. Boss -- lipstick
                 work Saturdays

    2. Friends -- no tennis   one fight
                  no fishing
                  "lover boy"

    3. Parents -- "cuddles"
               daughters of their friends
                   dinner? I didn't want?
      (Hers and mine)

         ⟶ Going "steady"

II   The Failure
    (not really being alone -- knowing "how"?)

A. Events
    1. Me -- shyness -- "responsibility"
    2. Others -- "kissing skills" -- fumble, knit,
                            purl --
    3. Breakup -- drifted -- "too busy" --
               no calls -- my move.

Later dates

B. Reaction
    1. Anger at self + her
    2. Jealousy -- others, whether they
                    existed or not
    3. Despair -- fishing + tennis, but
                others were busy w.
                Their own "loves"

III.   Aftermath

A. Triggering Events
  1. Airbase -- story
  2. Job -- husband arrives
  3. Death of mutual friend

B. Reaction
  1. How we handled it
  2. Her attitudes toward family
  3. my attitudes toward family
          (spouse/children)

[CONCL]
          She too, I realized, felt
  equally, undeniably "unreg-
  ulated."

    I think I can work from this outline. I set up my major Thesis points first: Obsession, Failure, Aftermath. Then, I decided to try grouping my material under illustrative subtopic headings of "Events" and "Reaction" (can you see the principle of Cause and Effect here?). Finally, I arranged my examples roughly in Temporal order, but also kept Ascending Importance in mind whenever the precise timing of detailed examples seemed not too important.

    Overall, you should note my increasing attention to *detail* where I have jotted phrases and words which will, I hope, produce the specific examples that will make my essay interesting.

As happened to me, so should you expect all of your Topic Outlines to undergo constant change. Any time during the structuring process you can add, delete, and adapt material in order to achieve proper balance, equal rank, and point back. It is while structuring, I believe, that time spent staring at your foul matter is most productive, because you'll waste *less* time at this stage of writing than you will later if your outline is faulty.

Once you start drafting an essay, you do not want to experience what some people call "writer's block," that period of empty despair when nothing comes, nothing gets put on paper. Creative artists writing fiction or drama often become blocked when they seem to run out of ideas for their characters' actions or thoughts; but for the kind of writing you will most probably be doing, a "block" should occur only if you find out too late that your structuring process has been improper or incomplete. If you have your Thesis and Topic Outline well prepared and developed, you will find that the actual writing of your essay will proceed if not always smoothly, at least with confident regularity.

Chapter 5

The Rough Draft

Let's see---- beginning -- last month, trip to New York, drove by

the corner of MillRiver Road and Rt. 35, wnating ti show wifex where

I ince lived. Turndoff once marked by Mobil Station sitting on ~~egde~~
egde

of open field, behind which was J----'s house. Not same. <u>Trees</u>

(set sultry scene -- Wolfe? "you can't go back again"?) -- no sign
                        protectively
of J---'s house -- trees enclosed new convenience story and Amoco

station, shletering, hiding everyhging.

                              as I returned from work
I missed the turnoff I had taken every summer day for two years.

Encarrassed, I explained to my wife that after all, things had changed
                        a slightly overweight
in thirty years. I had been 15x, not yet abbe legally to drive, and

had just started bb my first regular job.

Examine the above "paragraphs" carefully, please. They show a process which is more significant than the obvious fact that I've never taken a typing course. First—*and most important*—they are triple spaced. Never, never, *never* begin a rough draft by writing or typing on every line. I know, (as hundreds of students have told me) it's *hard* to break a lifetime habit of writing on every line—but you must. You should never again try to create a final copy when you start drafting a writing project, because just as an outline changes as it is conceived and developed, so does an essay change during the actual writing process. You are going to write bad sentences on your rough drafts. You are going to make errors in syntax and grammar. You are also going to write sentences, even paragraphs which are, well, all right by themselves, but when seen in the context of the entire draft, must be deleted, changed or moved around for clarity and emphasis. Even though you may feel uncomfortable in doing so, you must expect to slash, chop, cut, snip, and prune your rough drafts. Doing so may make you feel as if you are maiming your own child—after all, you and you alone created those words on the page—but the alteration job will have to be done. Triple spacing, whether you use pen, pencil or typewriter, will allow you almost enough room in which to work.

Second, my draft sentences and phrases that begin this chapter are choppy and riddled with errors and strikeovers. When you do a first draft, don't worry about fine points of grammar or syntax (as you become more polished as a writer, so will your drafts— some of the time). Working directly from your Topic Outline, just *write*. Let your words come. If you seem to stumble or become bogged down, leave a few blank spaces and start writing about your next point. You can always come back later.

Third, you can see that my sample draft paragraphs exhibit an identifiable progression: the initial phrases are choppy and dis-connected, but in the second paragraph, complete sentences appear. I begin all my non-fiction this way, having discovered some years ago that I was wasting more time on an introductory paragraph than on any other part of an essay. One day I realized why: an introductory paragraph points toward the essay, but how can something not yet written be properly introduced? Can you introduce two people whom you've never met? Neither can you write a proper introductory paragraph until you've at least writ-ten a draft. I actually write my introductory paragraphs immediately after drafting my conclusion, so that I can show the reader where the essay is going—just having been there myself.

My method of jotting free-flowing ideas for a scratch introduction is but one of many possible opening techniques. Some writers draft a conclusion first (I use this method for fiction), then work toward it. Others start midway through, drafting their Thesis Point #3 first, for instance, then doing #1 and #2. Regardless of what method best fits your writing habits, *never* write an introduction first, and always realize that the reading order of an essay is rarely the same as the order of writing it. Look at any house under construction: when is the front door added? Not in the beginning, certainly, even though that area is the first one you see when entering the house. Remember my comments on the "Blank Page Syndrome"? Trying to start by writing an introductory paragraph for a project you've not yet completed certainly helps create this problem.

When sentences begin to appear in my sample draft, you can see that I'm actually beginning to write, and if you'll look again at my outline on page 53, you'll see that I'm leading into point IA(1), "First Job—describe." What will follow in this and succeeding paragraphs are the details of that job. I want to make you *see* that gas station. I want to make you *feel* the heat on the concrete apron, and perhaps even *smell* the 40 gallons of gasoline I spilled one day when, distracted, I failed to note that the automatic cutoff nozzle had malfunctioned.

Note the above italicized words—they describe the senses of sight, touch, and smell. No matter what you write, always strive to appeal to as many of your reader's senses as possible. Joseph Conrad put it best: "My task which I am trying to achieve is, by the power of the written word to make you hear, to make you feel—it is, before all, to make you *see*. That—and no more, and it is everything."[1] Good advice for any writer. As you write your draft, consciously strive to use specific examples which create sensuous,[2] specific images for the reader.

Here are two examples. You can see the difference.

---

[1] "Preface" to *The Nigger of the Narcissus,* in *Three Great Tales,* New York: Modern Library, n.d., p. ix.
[2] You should know the difference between "sensuous" and "sensual."

Vague (25 words)	Sensuous-specific (25 words)
The Secretary of State, Alexander Haig, disagreed violently with Alexander Dobrynin, the Soviet Ambassador, who then decided to terminate the discussion and left the room.	After Soviet Ambassador Dobrynin growled "Nyet," Secretary Haig, slapping the table, snarled, "You don't want peace." Dobrynin jumped up, whirled, and marched out the door.

Here is my rough draft of the above examples. Note the changes.

```
          General                        Sensuous-Specific
       Alexander Haig              After
The Secretary of State disagreed    In Ambaddador DobryninXX smft smiling
       Alexander Dobrynin          and purred,          snarled
violently with the Soviet Ambassador "Nyet," Secretary Haig replied, "You
    then decided to terminate the   don;t want peace." When Haig slapped
who skrapkly bxxxskksxxkkxxxxxkxxgx xxxxxkxxbxxxxxg
                                    the table, Dobryning junomed im up,
discussionx and left thr room.                          marched
                        /          xpx spun about, and skxxpmxk out the

                                    doPb.
```

While this draft was in the typewriter, I made the immediate changes in words or phrases just after writing them—and there was enough space between lines to add material. Imagine my problem if I had started with a single-spaced draft. The other revisions were made later as I labored to create specifics and made the word count equal.

As you write your rough draft, do make *some* alterations as you go along, but don't make substantive revisions. Save major changes for later. Whenever you experience those perfectly normal slowdowns when you strain to get the right word, when the typewriter keys or the pen feels glued to the paper, or when you know that you've just written poorly, put a vertical line with an "X" opposite the offending words. Come back to them later. Here's an example from the revised draft on page 38 of this book:

The fourth possible organizational principle is that of Comparison and Contrast.

This one can be used whenever you are showing how a new process differs from an

older one, when you are writing about your company's ~~kaftxxxxxxx~~ sales record

being better or worse than a competitor's, or whenever you wish to show that

something is either like or unlike something else. (~~Today's~~ ~~xxxxxxxxxx~~ For young people, "first

love" is different from yesterday's because . . . . No, I don't want to write it

this way. When I was sixteen, I was really oblivious to my parents' ~~xxxxxxxxxx~~
perception of me — I was mainly interested in making

~~except to make~~ certain that they never really knew what I was doing. With

my own children, ~~I~~ all I know is what I can guess from what little they tell

me. Actually, I think there is little contrast, anyway. Reject this one.)

When comparing or contrasting,
Remember this distinction ~~phrase~~: you should compare like objects, and using

the phrase "compare with"; you should contrast unlike objects, using the

words "in contrast to."

If you compare this draft example with the finished page 38, you'll see that I decided to delete this personal comment which bothered me when I wrote it and which now seems even less relevant than it did then. Don't waste time as you go along beating a dying horse. Mark it, and when you go back to it, you'll probably find that it has expired by itself.

Your entire draft should resemble the two examples I have presented so far. When completed, your first draft should truly be a mess. Certainly, there will be paragraphs and pages which are more error- and strike-over-free than others: they represent the times when your prose was moving along nicely and you experienced that rare sense of creative fulfilment which made you actually enjoy writing—for a while. There will be too few of these moments, however.

Failure to understand that the first draft is still a malleable, rough precursor of the finished product is what keeps *most* inexperienced writers from realizing their potential. Once, after receiving supposedly rough drafts from a writing class of which over half had handed in neat, single-spaced first attempts on white paper, I waved the pages in front of the students and barked, "I don't care *what* first drafts look like. The messier the better. Write them on toilet paper for all I care." You can guess what I received for the next writing assignment. One student had filled an entire yellow roll of Scottissue. I have not made this suggestion since.

The Rough Draft, then, should be a relatively free-flowing exercise which in effect puts the first flesh on the skeleton of your Topic Outline. You should work directly from that outline, should keep your Thesis always in mind (and in sight), and should know not only what you have written but also what you are *going* to write about. During the writing of the first draft, you don't of course know exactly what you are going to *say* later on (that comes as you write), but if you have structured your essay properly, you will know the subtopics and many of the illustrations you are going to use. Therefore, you are able on occasion to guide the reader by foreshadowing or hinting at a future idea or reinforcing a previously stated point. For example, the second sentence of this paragraph restates the requirement of "keeping your Thesis always in mind." My outline contains a marginal note: "Stress *Thesis, Thesis, Thesis.*"

Many writing manuals spend quite a bit of time discussing paragraphs and sentences: The Topic Sentence; Paragraph Development; Transitions; Compound/Complex Sentences, and the like. I'll mention some of these topics too, but in the next chapter on Polishing. Experienced writers know that the Rough Draft is like the first molding of a clay figure—that the sharpness of features, the fine lines, the surface beauty (and yes, Transitions, complex constructions, and Topic Sentences) are often achieved during the slavework which *follows* the first, rough creation.

So it is with sentences, even paragraphs, whose excellence is usually insured in revision. After you have been at this writing game for a while, after you've learned why, how, and where to revise and rewrite, your first drafts will improve. I promise. For now, however, know that if you've outlined properly, if you've achieved the required balance of Thesis Statement, Subtopics, and Illustrations, that this general principle should apply: if you've got a good outline, you'll write good first draft paragraphs.

When writing your Rough Draft, remember these points:

Work from your outline.

Always triple (or at *least* double) space.

Do *not* start by writing the Introductory paragraph.

If you bog down, make a mark and go on.

Always keep Audience and Thesis in mind.

Concentrate on *details, details, details.*

One final suggestion: if your writing project is too extensive for you to complete a draft in one sitting, always quit in the middle of an idea, even in the middle of a sentence. Never take a break after finishing a complete thought, a paragraph, a section, or a chapter, because if you do effect this kind of completion you may have difficulty getting going when you get back. Instead, what you should do is this: (I have a dental appointment in an hour, so I'll stop writing this draft now—)

① Check outline

② jot notes ahead for the idea you have left unfinished

③ start draft of "Love" essay

(Re-read all)

The notes reproduced above are the ones I wrote to myself yesterday afternoon, just before leaving for the dentist. Regardless of the reason, when you must interrupt your writing for a while, you should stop at a point where you know exactly what you want to say next. Check your outline, then jot on your draft page a couple of notes for the next day's writing. These notes will assist you to get going again—without sitting and staring. Little warmup is required, because you're already in gear and ready to move.

If your break has been a substantial one (overnight, for instance), start by rereading everything you've so far written, but again, make only minor alterations or corrections before continuing your rough draft. If you see the need for major surgery, make a note. Don't start rewriting your first paragraph, for instance, or you may never be able to get away from it. Your main job now is to get your rough draft done.

My main job now is to show you what a rough draft looks like. Here goes. I am checking the time: 9:28 AM. I'll start where I left off at the beginning of this chapter. Subtopic #1: "The Obsession."

Pumping gas was not my idea of a career, but I needed the money. I

had walked Into the two-pump, paint peeling Mobil Station the week

                                  behind ~~xxxdarkxxxbxgkxxxx~~
previous and asked the old man who was alone ~~inxthexxkxttxexd~~

the soptted glass case if he needed some help. He looked about 75 --

                denim
was waering a stanied trainman's cap, and needed a shave. "Can't pay

      "You a mechanic?" I told him I knew a little about engines.
much," he said. "You got working papers?" I told him I was fifteen.

"Can't even pay <u>that</u> much then," he said. We settled on 75¢ an hour. I
                                I would work 5 days and have
would start the next day for a week's ~~tratk~~ trial. "Then I'll see," he *Mondays*
                                       and
                                     Tuesdays
said.
                                       off.

      ~~Tnak 2~~ Usually, all I did was pump gas, check and add oil, and
~~NxxxStxxxx~~

change a few tires. I was Mr. Simms' first hired man, and he seemed to take

little interest in me. His pumps were the pre World War II kind with the

                        was no
glass bubble on top, and there ~~wxxx~~ no hydraulic lift in the one

                     dark and
car bay -- just a pit which was slippery from ~~gx~~ what I suspected was

                                 In side the glass case
a thirty-year accumulation of oil pan drippings. ~~Inxtxffixxt~~

which filled half of the tiny"office" was an assortment of old candy bars,

cans of oil additive (some of which were rusted on top), some fan belts,

car waxes whose labels I had never neen before, and a few roadmaps of

Maine, North Carolina, and other (to me then) faraway places.

On my first day, Mr. Simms left for "lunch" at noon. He did not

return until amoust four. Ixbmd There had been only fmmx six customers, ③

I think, and two or three others who had stopped fmx to ask directions. ←exploring station

                                        in the threadbare arm chair
No problems, I told my obviously beery boss. He sat down behind the glass

case. "Good," he said. "Go home. Se you in the morning." I wondered

if he noticed kmncxkxxxxkkmx that ẍ He could see through the glass.

Most of the days were similar to that first one. Very little
        Tmxubxyx

business, just enough, I calculated, to pay fmxxxyxxmxxkxmx my wages and

leave about an equal amount for Mr. Simms. Occasionally, such as on the

July 4th holiday weeked, we would see a rush --but usually there would be

only four or five customers and hour, none of whom seemed"regular." Mxxxxxxs

There were no kxxgxxxxxxxxx appointments for grease jobs or oil changes,

no requests for tuneups or tires -- just gas, and off the customer would go.

Abht the only regularity was the lngth of Mr. Simms's lucnh hour -- and

it was not long beofre I realized that the major reason he had hired me was

to give himself a break from the chores, he once told me, he had been doing

sold his livery stable in 1921.
since he had ~~xkxxgxxbxfxxxxqxxfxxxxxxxxxxxxxxx~~

Consequently, I had time on my hands -- so I ~~spxxx~~ began cleaning up the

station, inside and out. I pulled ~~wxxxx~~ the weeds which had come from the

beyond which I could see a few nwer houses
three acre vacant lot to the north, ~~bxxxxxx~~ which were a

through the trees. I shined the ~~xx~~ pumps and mowed the small island between

 patched
the asphalt of the apron and the road. I began starighetening up the   ④

greasy bay area, throwing out pieces of metal which I did not recognize,

uncovereing a scredriver here, a wrench there which I replaced in the

~~gxxxx~~ crusty tool box which, when cleaned in the oil dripping pan, shone a dull

belts
gunmetal gray. I arranged the fan ~~bxxxx~~ by size along one wall as I had

seen in others stations, noticing that there wrere many small ones and large

ones, but few in the most popular sizes. I swept, polished, dusted and

reaagganged, taking a hasty inventory in case Mr. Simms ever wanted to order
customer
half a dozen requests for ~~x~~ popular candy,
anything. And finally, after ~~bxxxbxxxxxxxxxxxxxxxxxxxxxxxxxxxx~~ I even

ordered a new supply of cany bars from a wholesaler who happened to stop ~~bxx~~

by and restacked the glass case. The Hershey, Snickers, and Baby Ruth barsx

~~xxxxxxxxxxx~~ looked colorful through the clear glass of the case.

As I was admiring this new display, a ~~xxxxx~~ female voice behind me said,

"Ill take a Hershey bar, please." Startled, I turned and saw her for the

first time. ~~Xxxxxxxx~~ Mediuxm lenghth dirty blonde hair tied in a pony tail.

Thin lips with bright red lipstick framing ~~xxxxxxxxxxxx~~ slightly crooked

    white

teeth. Man's button-down shirt with rolled-up sleeves. Red shorts.

Sneakers. About my age, I remember thinking. ~~xxxxxxxx~~ Because she

was standing on the asphlat and I was one step up in the doorway, she seemed

very short. "Hi," she said. "I'm Marian. I live over there." She

po nted across the vacant lot. *"I've been watching you."* (5)

  Yes, ~~xxxxxxxx~~ I felt flushed. Yes, my heart pounded. And yes,

           Driven by one or the other set of parents,

I fell in love immediately. ~~xxxxxxxxxxxxxxxxxxxxxxx~~

I had taken girls to movies. I had played tennis with them. I had

danced with them at arranged school functions. I had ~~xxxxxxxx~~ listened

to my younger sister's friends giggling ~~xxx~~ in her room long into the

night. And I had traded boasts with my own firnds about how experienced

I was with girls, ~~xx~~ but except for one inept kissing experience ~~xxxx~~

in the woods with a gril whose name I've forgotten, I was as ignornat

about women as I now realize most of my boasting friends were, too.

Here, unannounced, unexpected, was a pretty girl who had said that she

was "watching me."

  I sodl her a Hershey bar and we began what would be many conversations.

During Mr. Simms's three-hour lunch that day, and on most of the

susequent days, we talked in that tiny office about music, books (she liked to read and had just started The Naked and the Dead, and which she said

with a wink that she kept hidden under her bed because of the language).

She did not play tennis, nor did she ski -- but she loved to swim. We could

go down to the river, she suggested. I knew the pool. I tried to imagine her

in a bathing suit. I liked the thought. Movies? Of course. Perhaps her

older brother could drive sometime, and we could go up to Danbury where there

was a new outdoor theatre where we could sit in the car. Another wink.

That first conversation, with me sitting in the old chair and Marian

                                              or
walking up and down on the other side of the case leaning against it

(her red shorts were about the same color os the detail on the Baby

Ruth wrappers) was one of the most breathless discussions I have ever

had. She seemed so poised, so vivacious, so much in control, while I

                                              I even
tripped over my tongue, kept clearing my throuat, and once forgot the title

of the movie which I has jst admitted to seeing three times. When the first

customer interrupted my idyll by honking his horn angrily, I bolted out

of the chair and banged my knee on the side of the glass case. Marian

giggled, and I hoped as I filled the Buick's tank that my face did not look

too flushed. After that, Marian sat in the ciar and I hovered by the door,

knowing that is she were seated behind the case there was less chance of a

customer's seeing her.

At abour three o'clock, she got up, walked aroun to where I was standing,

and put her hand on my arm. I tingled. "I'd beet go," she said. "Old Simms

might come back early." So she had really been watching, I thought. "See

you tomorrow." Part way across the open field, she turned and blew me a

kiss.

⚹ Thᵢs my first infatuation began -- with a rᵢquest for a candy bar --

and it lasted for almost ~~two years~~. Marian would come over almost

every day, shortly after Mr. Simms would leave. S̶t̶x̶x̶x̶x̶d̶x̶b̶x̶x̶x̶d̶x̶x̶ ⑦

M̶X̶X̶ From her side porch she could see his x̶x̶x̶ 1939 Ford chug its way x̶x̶x̶

down x̶x̶x̶ Route 35 toward Ridgefield, and within half an hour, there she would

be, usually dressed in shorts, sometimes with her shirt tied halter

fashion, often x̶x̶x̶x̶ carrying a paper bag with her lunch (and sometimes a

sandwich for me). Occasionally, she would bring a book which she would read

while I was putside, trying to concentrate on my job.

That summer, I saw Marian at least six days a week. ⊠⊠⊠⊠⊠⊠⊠⊠⊠⊠⊠⊠⊠⊠

On Modays and Tuesdays, we would swim, bicycle somewhere for a picnic,

or play tennis (she wanted to learn -- to have _me_ teach her) at a nearby

court. Some days, we would spend the aftrenoon at each others' houses,
_{or evening}

with our mothᵢrs always present but not visible. We would read, listen to
_{obviously}

the radio, or talk. That summer, I don;t recall ever seeing my brother or sister, nor do remember doing anything with my parents. Everything was

Marianx, ~~Myxxxxxxxxxx~~ such was my obsession with her. After about a month,

we cpnfessed our love for each other, and ~~xx~~ I knew that what we had

together was irrevocable, permanent, and unique. No one had ever loved

anyone   as strongly or as completely as I did Marian.

    Of course, we did more than talk. We fumbled, touched, kissed,

explored, ~~xxxxxxxxx~~ nibbled, and seemed forever trying to catch our

    breaths. We used the word "frustration" a lot, and I learned how

to say "No!" with ~~xxxxxxxxxxxx~~ fatalistic yearning. Once, when
                       entire
we thought my parentswere out for the evening, we went upstairs to my room,

but before anyhthing could develop, the sound of tires in the gravel driveway

brought us racing down the steep stairs, just in time. My mother had forgotten

her purse. We decided that to try that again would be too risky.

    In August, I received my drivers' license -- and whenever I could pry

my father's car loose, Marian and I transferred our ~~fxxxkxxgs~~ breathlessness
  seat   in
to the front (never ~~xxx~~ back, she said). That we always "stopped," I think,

was a result of fear, ignorance, and what we did not recognize then as

a ~~xxxxxx~~ budding sense of resonsibility. We were afraid, or course,

of pregnancy; we were ignorant, basically, of not what to do but of exactly

how to do it; but most important, we did have a sense that ~~xxxxxxxxx~~ a complete sxual relationship carried with it some responsibilities that we

were not, despite our feeling so mature, ready to handle. I think now,

looking back, that we really liked each other. Perhaps that ~~xxxx~~ fact was

                              we preferred frustration to consummation.
the reason that ~~xxxxxxxxxxxxxxxxxxxxxxxxxxxxxxxxxxxxxxxxx~~

~~xxxxxxxxxxxxxxxxxxxxxxx~~in   I
    Althoughk our world ~~xxxxxxxx~~ consisted of each otjer, ~~xx~~ could not help

noticing some reactions from ~~xxxxxx~~ other peopale. Mr. Simms, for **i**nstance,
suggested
~~told me~~ late one afternoon that

                              Stopped: 11:30; started: 8:48

                                                                    (9)

I'd better check my face in the mirror before ~~xxxxxxxxxx~~ the next customer

came. In the cracked mirror of the only bathroom, I saw the lipstick

on my left cheek. ~~I~~ As I bolted by him, face averted and obviously red, I

wondrered if he were smiling. He never said ~~xxxxxxxxxx~~ anything else; nor

did he change his schedule, but we were much more carefule after that.

    My parents, too, began to take notice. One evening after ~~xxxx~~ dinner,

my mother asked me ~~xxx~~ if I'd be interested in taking the daughter of a frinend

of hers to a movie the following night. I said no. A few days later,

at breakfast, she ~~xxxxxxxxxxxxxxxxxxxx~~ told me that I was invited to a

picnic which would just happen to take place on my next day off. I

declined that ~~x~~ obviously contirved, I thought then, opportunity, ~~xxxx~~ too.
It also seemed to me that she stayed home more often, espeically when I
~~xxxxxxxxxxx~~
was not aorking.

more
Marian's parents as well~~z~~ seemed to take interest in ~~xbxixxmxxmexm~~ our

closeness. Because her mother worked, Marian's day was unstructured, but

she began to have a few evenings taken up with "family" matters, she told

me, and her cousins ~~xxd~~ seemed to arrive unexpectedly on my days off. Once,

                                                          xx
she was gone for a week with her mother and father, and ~~ixdmegxmxdxxxxxpxxx~~

becaise they had never taken a ~~f~~ "family" vacation before, we began to suspect

a d~~i~~ne plot.

TRAND: (10)

        The great insult came one evening at diiner when my father, a brandy

in hand, looked at his watch and asked me ~~xby~~ whether I was seeing

"Cuddles" that night. My mother looked a bit stricken. My sister choked into

                                                       had to live
her napkin. I glared at all of them, these people with~~t~~ whom I ~~kxxmt~~

and ~~xbxxi~~ whom I suddenly hated. Obvioully, they had been talking about us

behind our backs. "I don;t know what you're talking about," I announced

pompously, then rushed from the table to ~~pxbxk~~ pout for a while in the

sancticty of my room.

        My ~~fix~~ friends, too, seemed to recede into the distance. Early in

the summer, boys I had gone to school with for years would call to set up

a softball game, some tennis, some fisbing afternoons, but by the middle

of August, the calls became rare. I had run out of excuses. Because I

                                                   already
was slightly younger than most of my classmates, I had ~~xdxys~~ shared ~~tbxxfbx~~

their driver's license sprees; and when mine came, there was only Marian.

When I did see some of my friends in town, they would seem friendly enough

but distant, and once when someone asked how my love life was going, I felt

the same anger ~~xxxix~~ that had possessed me after my father's joke. The

crisis erupted one day in front of the drugstore when three friends

converged on me, said their greetings, and asked if I wanted to go camping

the following Monday. "~~X~~He can;t," one said. "He's working." The other

two smirked~~x~~ and shook their heads. "No he's not," one said. "He'll be

~~hxcixgxxx~~ playing kissy-face with Marian." I tried to hit him, but someone caughmt

my arm, and the three of them walked slwoly away, not looking back, leaving

me alone on the hot ~~xxxxxx~~ streetconrner.

At the end of summer, before Marian and I had to go back to our respective

schools, a hundred miles apart, I ~~xxkxxd~~ told her that of course we were going

steady, weren't we, and that we would have to write a lot of letters and

that it would be a lonely fall. I'd try to get down to see her, but because I

didn;t have a car, I did not know when. I think that we were parked someonwhere

after a movie. Her reaction surprised me, because it was the first time I had

seen her appear hesitant. She loved me, she said, really, but no -- we weren't

really going steady. Her mother wouldn;t allow it. I exploded, telling her

~~that~~ what did parent~~ix~~ know, our business was our business, and that if she loved me, she'd go steady anyway. She drew back as far as she could

on the seat, looked at me and said slowly, "I can't." After the silence which

followed, our brathlessness seemed more intense than ever, and we decided

ix (no, <u>she</u> decided and I reluctantly agreed) that we were as good as going

steady, even if we weren't.

That fall saw a great exchange of letters, each of us professing

loneliness, xixkxx frustration, and undying love. There would never be anyone

else, we vowed. Aikkxxgk We were xxxxixg refusing all xxkxxx opportunities

for dates, and xxxkxxkxx anyway, we hadn;t so much as seen anyone else

who might matter. I certainly had not, although there were one or two

dances which I'd attended, and once, when a girl I'd been dancing with

suggested that we walk outside where it was cooler, I refused stiffly

and told her that I was committed. I know now that the particular xxix
                that
angle xf her eyebrow assumed in response was the universal sign for

her realization that I was, at least for the moment, a real jerk.

XX When Christmas vacation started, I arrived hxme first and insisted

upon meeting her train. I remember calling her parents and announcing
                Mariah
that I would pick kxx up, and I assumed that they would not be there.

I was wrongx then, too. I had not noticed them standing to one side
                                                the
and as Marian stepped down from a rear car, kxx fxr collarxxkxxxxkx of her

coat barely covered by ~~xxxxxxxxxxxxxxxxxxxx~~ a new page boy haircut,

I raced toward her, only to see her smile and wave and then trow her arms around

her mother -- before I could get there. I got to carry her suitcase to

her father's car.

                                                      evening
The next night (she had to be with her family, that first ~~night~~), I

knew that something had changed. There was something about her, something

about the way she moved, the way she tossed her shorter hair, the way she,

well, kissed, that was not the same. We said all the same words, of course,

but something was different. Our second date, another movie, resulted

in ~~x~~ my feeling more uneasiness, and the third time we were together,

I decided to ask her. I scratched for the right words, then blurted,

"You kiss differently."

    "I what?" she said.

    "You kiss differently," I repeated.

    She replied, somewhat diffidently, that she really din;t know what I

meant, but I <u>knew</u>. I also knew <u>she</u> knew. I aksed her if there was anyone else.

She replied of course not, not really, and when I aksed her what "not

really" meant, she shrugged her shoulders and answered, "Nothing." Then

she added, "Anyway, you kiss differently too.X So what."

    I don;t remember what else we said that night, but I do know that

                                                her
the evening ended dismally. I saw only once again that vacationx (her

                      for a week
parents took her skiing and did not invite me), and I with adolescent

frenzy called up everyone I had known, went to a number of parties,

made a lot of promises to every girl I met, and generally tried not to

                                                         party
feel sorry for myself. Our last date was a disaster -- a ~~dance~~ at which

she seemed to know everyone, and more tragic, everyone seemed to know her.

                                    in corners of a room
I observed her talking two or three times to other young men, ~~xxxxxxxxxx~~

one of whom ~~knox~~ was even a former friend of mine, and I think I drank

two or three beers more than I should have from the supply of the hosts

liberal parents. I'm not certain whetehr I even kissed Marian goodnight.

     When I returned to school, I fumed for some time. Obviously, Marian had

lied to me. She had been dating all fall, I knew, sharpeing her kissing

skills. I had been stupid, ~~xxxxxx~~ of course, all that previous summer,

too. I had been just one of many. That's what my firend's phrase ~~xxxxx~~

"good old Marian" meant. Perhaps one of **them** had even been **him.** What else

had she done with them that she hadn;t done with me? What had she been
doing all fall? With whom? How often?
                          and
     My anger, jealousy, ~~and despair~~ lasted well into March, even though

~~xxxxx~~ Marian and I exchanged letters which seemed little different than

before. I could not bring myself to mention what I was really thinking,

and her correspondence indicated that she either did not know how I felt or that she did not care. She looked forward to the summer, she said, when

she too could drive, and was I going to work at the gas station again?

She couldn;t wait.

I'll bet, I thought. ~~XX~~ And I fumed some more. Finally, in late

March, I wrote the letter which vented all my pent-up fury. It was about

ten pages, I think, and I told her that our relationship could never last unless

she stopped ~~k~~lying to me, told me everything, and promised never to do it again.

(15)

I waited until ~~Aprik~~ the middle of April for the reply which never came.

When I tried to call her three times, the girl at the desk of her dormitory

said she was out. I wrote a follow-up letter, modifying my position

graciously, I thought, and begging her to write. She never did.

~~Thxixerxdcocoomx~~
In June, when I started work again at the same gas station (MR. Simms

                                   reacuried
looked the same, and the glass case had ~~xxxxxx~~d its blotched appearance),

                                        for the first twom weeks
my anger and jealously had abated, but what replaced it was despair.

I tried to call Marian, but twice her mother said that she couldn;t come to

the phone. The third time, when I insisted upon talking to her, Marian

told me that we really shouldn;t see each other, at least not for a whil e,

that we should just be firends. That was it. So I would go to the

little Mobil Station each day, try not to look too often acroos the field

where I knew <u>she</u> was, and clean, snip, polish and prune with a frinzy, wondering if she were watching. ᴀ̶f̶t̶e̶r̶ᴡ̶a̶r̶d̶ In the third week of my summer

vacation, I met Anne, and although I knew without qualification that

it could never be the same again, I mnaged to fall quickly in love for

the second time.

    Because we moved that fall, and because when I graduated from

college I joined the Air Force, I did not ᴇ̶ᴠ̶ᴇ̶r̶ᴍ̶a̶r̶i̶a̶n̶ think I would ever see

Marian again. Ten years later, however, while shopping in the Base

Commisary for my family which now included three small children, I s̶ᴇ̶ᴇ̶x̶

wheeled a loaded cart around a corner and collided with an extremely   (16)

pregnant woman who just shook her head at me and smiled. "You're still

bumping into things, aren't you," she said. It was Marian carrying, she

told me later as we talked in the parking lot, her fourth child. Her

                                  the
husband was a student pilot in s̶q̶u̶a̶d̶r̶o̶n̶ squadron which worked opposite hourse

         in which   and would be graduating in a month.
to the one I was instructing. We would have to get together, she said,

to talk about old times.

    We never did. That night at home, with my wofe wondering what

on earth was the matter, I started to write again, this time a short

story about a young man's first love. T̶h̶r̶e̶e̶x̶ I finished it three days

later, and when I showed it to my wife̶ᴘ̶ᴏ̶ᴇ̶ᴍ̶ and told her̶

                          my
what had coused t̶h̶i̶s̶x̶creative resurgence, she said only that she didn;t

think she and Marian would have much in common and that anyway, hadn;t

I said that instructors and students should mingle socially? As with

                                   about my wife
my relationship with Moarian, I think I understand more now than I did

then, but I realized thatx at least that pressing for a reunion would

                     decided to bring up the subjext
be difficult, and by the time I broughtxxx the subject again, Mroian's

husband had already graduated and had been assigned to Germany. I had

of course checked with instructor friends of mine in his squadron. He was

a good guy and a good pilot. I felt happy for her. (17)

    By the time I saw her again, I had divorced,xxx remafried, and had

been reassigned often. It was her husband, now a Major, whon I talked

with first x when he reopted in to my departemt at the United States Air Firce

Academy. He knew all about me, he said, Marian had told him (I wondred even

then -- how much?), and as soon as they werr settled, we'd get toghter.

    We did. There were Department functions, an occasional small dinner

party, and an occasional picnic or two -- but somehow we never seemed to

have the opportunity to talk about thexxx the good old days at all. I

came to respect Marian's husband; we flew together often and taught

similar calsses; and fxxxxxxxxxxxxxxxxxxxxxxxxxxxxxxxxxxx our wtves

    at least
became social, if not really close friends. Ocassioanlly, I would ask

Marian about her parents and she would inquire about mine, but for the most part our relationship was identical to those experienced by most couples

who share similar jobs and lifestyles. I liked their children; they liked

ours, and except for the ties of ~~place~~ birthplace, we seemed to have

only superficial ties in common. Then ~~her~~ Marian's husband was transferred,

and I did not see them again for two years.

The cause of our last meeting was the death of a very close mutual

friend. Marian's husband was stationed at the same base; we had both known

Tony Dater as the prince that he was; and when I heard that he had been killed

in a crash, I had to be there. Marian's husband called. I, and the others

who ~~would~~ were coming in for the funeral, would stay with them.

When I stepped out of my aircraft into the 100° heat of Big Spring, Texas,

                                  concrete
there was ~~Madison~~ Marian, standing on the ramp below the exit ladder just as she

had stood by the gas station door, twenty-eight years before. She drove

to their quarters and we held hands and cried all the way. ~~Every~~ We had

all loved Tony very much.

Later that night, after the exhausting process of handling affairs

for the funeral, talking with family and friends, ~~xxxxx~~ and meeting new

artovals, Marian and I talked until nearly dawn. Perhaps it was the

emotional release afforded by the death of a friend or parhaps it was

just time to do so, but we relived that summer and fall, day by day,

~~innit~~ indident by incident, and we laughed and cried and held hands, and

by morning, everything was all right. Marian's husband had gone to bed

early; there was another friend sleeping on the living room couch just

a few feet away from where we sat; but nothing disurbed us at all.

No, she said, she had not been carrying on with anyone else that fall --

EMPH in rewrite --concl.

well, she said smileing the way she had so often, (not really.) Nothing

serious. Hadnlt <u>I</u> been? No? She was surprised. She thought I had.

Yes, my letter had hurt her very much, and she had thrown away ~~the~~ unread

(19)

one which followed. Yes, she <u>had</u> watched me for the first two weeks of

thinking of

the folloing summer, and had been ~~xxxxxxxxxx~~one over when she heard about

Anne -- who was so much prettier than she was. I disputed that, and

we laughed some more. Yes, that night when my mother came ~~xxxx~~ back

unexpectedly had been terrifying. No, she had not been as close ~~xx~~ as

she had been with me ~~xxxxxx~~ with anyone else until after we broke up.

~~xxxxxxxxxx~~ No, I had never told her about Mr. Simms' remark about the

lipstick. And on, and on, and on.

We also talked about the present and near past, about our familes,

our children (we each had fifteen-year-olds who were exhibiting the same

Her

silly symptoms ~~that~~ as we had), and our general mistakes and fears.

thoughts.

(more)

had been

We agreed that given the standards of today, ~~xx~~ our realtionship ~~xxx~~

really quite innocent, and that despite our individual sense of

fristration at the time, fun. Not idyllic, but for the moast part --

fun. Most important, I think, we agreed that our experience had served

to caution us not to interfere with our own children when they too

would fxxxx so obviously fxxxxxxx be experiencing those first love

depressions and fears, and as I fell asleep, I remember Marians

hand and her last statement; "You know," she said," I really love my

husband." I told her that I really loved my wife. "But," she said,

"I love you too." "Me too," I said. Then I fell asleep.

Marian too, I know now, had felt just as unrequited as I had, and

for xxxx many of the same reasons. She had been as obsessed with me as I had

been with her; she had felt the similar twinges when we had so

unpredictably met; and shex too xxxxxxx believed that everything

had worked out for the best, that our mutual first love had helped us gxxx

do more than just grow up. We exchange Christmas cards now; our children

are gxxxxxxx starting familes of their own; and we have no regrets.

Well -- I suppose -- as Marian would say, not really. *stopped: 11:04*

(Total time so far on essay: 4 hrs, 18 min)

There's a rough draft, one that turned out much longer than I had anticipated. I feel somewhat drained, but before I look this draft over, I want to do two necessary chores: first (I've been keeping some notes as I wrote), I want to write on draft page 18 a reminder to emphasize Marian's phrase "not really" in order to lead up to the concluding sentence, and second, I must write the draft of the introductory paragraph.

Here it is:

INTRO

We were parked on the side of Route 35 south of Firfield, Conn. It was over there, I told my wife, where Marian's house ~~inx~~ was.

My wife
~~She~~ said that she couldn;t see anything. The trees were too thick~~x~~   maple and oak

          I remembered as
,~~MX~~ in what ~~knxboxxxxxxxbxxn~~ a vacant field. This must be the corner, I thought,

even though what used to be a small, ~~xkntkxxframxx~~ dirty-white frame

Mobil ~~Stxxkkxxx~~ station was now ~~x~~ ~~Sxkx~~ self-serve AMOCO convienience store.

~~Everything~~ was so ~~kuch~~ more open, I told my wife, when I worked there. She

said that she knew. I had told her the story~~xxxxx~~ about Marian, she ~~dxxxx~~
                                        July
added. ~~Abiut~~ the only similarity was the heat which made both if us feel

sticky.

     "Want to see where I used to live," I ~~asked.xxxx~~ She said sure, why
          especially   though.
not. She didn;t want to see Marian's house, ~~shxxxxxkxx~~. We were running late.

     Beacuse trees ~~kxxbxxxxxxxxxx~~ shielded the sign, I missed the turnoff

I had taken every day that summer ~~x~~ when I walked home from work.
                                                          right
~~ExkxxxxxxxxxpdxxbxxxdxxbxxxxqxxkxxUxtxxxx~~and this time found the road. ~~Texxxx~~

```
Thirety-three years beofre, Ixкхolxbsenx a slightly plump fifteen-year-old,

I had found my first regualr job as a gas station attendant, and shortly

after that, I had met and fallen in love with Marian.  Pumping -----------
```

There's an introduction, and I'm not particularly happy with it. What I'm going to do, however, is place it with the rest of the draft, sharpen some pencils, and start the slavework. Writing the rough draft, as I hope you will find out soon, is easy and fun—compared with what has to be done later.

Chapter 6

Writing Under Pressure: Timed Examinations and Other Required Indignities

---

AS I HAVE IMPLIED SO FAR, most teachers or supervisors assume that you should have enough time to write, if only you plan correctly. Often not mentioned in class or in writing manuals, however, are those writing requirements which will plague you in one form or another for the rest of your life. I refer to those pressure times when the boss needs that report *yesterday,* when you check your calendar and discover that you've forgotten a two-o'clock deadline, or when someone tells you that the district manager is coming in this afternoon—and wants to see your new ideas in writing. For students, these pressure times usually occur at the end of each semester with final examinations, but there are also mid-terms, hour exams, pop quizzes, and of course those too frequent occasions when one just forgets when a written assignment is due.

Writing under pressure within a specific, usually short time limit is basically no different than writing at leisure: the steps and principles are the same. You must, however, adapt the Basic Law of Good Writing to better allow you to make the most of your restricted time.

Here's how you should revise the Law:

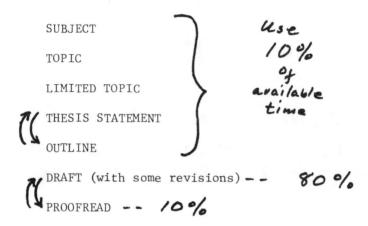

Note the differences from the Law as expressed earlier on page 5. You should use this adapted Law whenever you realize that there absolutely is not enough time to write more than one draft. Remember always: what you do *not* want to be doing when your time is up is to be writing frantically, throwing out those last minute ideas which you forgot to include earlier.

Consider that the process of writing under pressure is similar to flying an airplane: you can go just so far on one tankful of gas and no more. *Don't* try to do too much.

You can improve your pressured writing by following a prearranged timed procedure. Using the steps of the Basic Law *in order,* allot at least ten percent of your time to create Thesis and Outline, about eighty percent to write a legible draft, and at least ten percent to proofread and make necessary, neat corrections on that draft. For instance, if your examination has an hour-long essay question, plan to spend six minutes planning and at least six minutes proofreading. This process leaves you only 48 minutes in which to write—more than enough time if you do it right. If your exam starts at 2:00, conceive and structure until at least 2:06, stop writing *no later* than 2:54, and check your work for the remainder of the time. I'll repeat: do *not* still be writing when the bell rings.

Usually, material presented during a last-minute scribbling is nothing more than verbal vomit and adds nothing to your paper.

Likewise, if you finish with a fine conclusion before your time is up, stop. Use your blessed extra minutes to revise some internal sentences and to include a few more facts in the body of your essay. Don't merely add sentences at the end just to make your work seem longer; doing so will make your essay resemble a tadpole and will rarely improve the value of your work.

For the inexperienced writer, these pressure situations almost always produce the after-the-fact comment, "I could have written a whole book, if only I'd had time." What this statement really means is this: "I didn't plan my writing project properly." The perpetrator of the timed indignity—teacher, boss, supervisor—*knows* that you can't write a book in an hour, and if you try to do so, it's your fault alone if your project fails.

If you limit properly, achieve Thesis and a Thesis Statement, and write a useful Scratch Outline, you will be able to present an organized, well-developed, detailed essay which not only "answers the question" but also pleases the reader.

Here's an example:

> Question: In a twenty-five minute short essay, show how the media have affected the youth in America since World War II.

(What a question! I would not ask this of my students; but it is similar to one I once saw on an American Studies examination.) Here goes. I'm timing myself.

*   *   *

24.5 minutes later: it *was* a ridiculous question. Here is how I went about answering it: first I noted the stop time at the top of a scratch page; then I jotted these notes and the accompanying scratch outline. Notice how I struggled with Thesis, after limiting to TV and perception and deciding to use examples from my own experience.

Stop: 3:58

Subj - MEDIA

L.top → Books   Radio   TV

Not read   Music + driving   Sex   Sound

Perception

① Perception -- real + unreal

My children

A - bird v. cartoon but

B - "slaughter" - actors

C - "Let's watch war"

Intro - Crime? Values? Politics

Thesis -

~~The effect of TV on American~~ *affected*
~~How TV has helped~~
~~a generation of American children~~
~~distort reality to exemplify~~ *exemplifies*
My children's reaction to TV exemplifies
Their generation's distortion of reality
because of the bird incident, the
actor question, and their reaction to
The Vietnam war.

Then I wrote the following essay. The changes I made during the last two minutes are indicated in heavier ink. Notice the relatively neat strikeovers, the changes, and especially the technique used for the last sentence of paragraph #2. While writing my answer, I bogged down here, not being able to think of another specific example to illustrate my point about people

having difficulty believing what they see. I left a blank; then went
back afterward and filled it in.

Much has been written about

the Media (Books, Newspapers, Radio, TV) and

their effect upon American values. *TV,*
however, seems to have received the most attention.
Changing attitudes toward sex and violence,

even toward the family itself have

all been accounted for in terms of

our young people's ~~exposure~~ obsession

with ~~TV, for movies,~~ **"the tube."**

There is a reason, I think, ~~which~~

~~underlies~~ for TV's effect, one which

underlies and causes most of the problems

of our young people **face** ~~cause~~ -- and have to
deal with.
~~face~~

I refer to the change in perception which TV has produced in its younger viewers, a change which ~~you~~ seems to have resulted in an inability to distinguish between the real and the unreal. People used to believe at least what they saw -- but now, many of them are not so sure even of that. Witness those who believe former President Nixon was "railroaded," or that a certain mouthwash _does_ kill bacteria, even though published studies say no.

The source of this problem is the medium itself. When my daughter was about two, for instance, I saw her watching a cartoon on Saturday morning. To the right of the TV set was an open window that ~~stood~~ framed a tree branch on which a robin sat, preening. The TV screen also ~~framed~~ a cartoon bird, and I suddenly realized that my daughter was looking from one scene to the other -- from the present to the real bird, wondering, evaluating, comparing.

What she may have been thinking was ~~exemplified~~ later by a comment her older sister made after watching (without my knowledge) a particularly violent show. "How do they get all those

acious to let people such brains in Them,"
my five-year-old asked. I replied that
it was all fake, that she didn't have to
worry. "Oh," she replied. "I thought it was
real."

The perception problem was best summed up by
a comment from my six-year-old son, who years later
appeared agitated one night at dinner. He
keeps asking what time it was, and
finally said, "Hurry, daddy -- we'll miss
The War." What he was referring to
was the nightly CBS news — a "factual" show. To him, the
intense coverage of the Vietnam battle
scenes resembled his older sister's

cartoons: unreal, adventuring, some or fictional.

These Three examples are small ones, true -- but They showed provide a warning to those of us who have not always had TV in the house. When we wonder why our children don't seem to understand the difference between right and wrong, good and evil -- perhaps it's in part because Their perception of the real and unreal has been blurred by the sheer ~~fact~~ of television itself. Quite an impact indeed.

The reader of an essay written under pressure does not expect polished perfection, but that reader will require that you show an ability to organize, develop, and use supporting detail. If you develop a precise system for writing, you can adapt that system to examinations and last-minute projects, and when you stop writing, even though your fingers will be no less cramped than ever, you will have written much better indeed.

Chapter 7

POLISHING: Revising, Rewriting, Proofreading

AS DID CHAPTER 5, this one begins with an example, here, one of the Revised Drafts for page 1 of *Writing From Scratch:*

ChapTer 1

~~SECTION I~~

The Basic Law of Good Writing

law: 1. all the rules of conduct ~~established and enforced by the authority~~ . . . . 6. ~~all such rules~~ having to do with a particular sphere of human activity.

Webster's New World Dictionary

You're reading This book because you want to improve your writing. Start now -- by learning The Basic Law of Good Writing

The difference between this law and ~~all others~~ any others you know is quite simple: you ~~can enforce~~ are the ~~only person who can enforce it and make it work for you.~~ If you do, you'll

be ~~on your way to~~ writing well. If you don't, you'll continue to muddle along as you have -- ~~probably~~ being too infrequently ~~suprising~~ surprised ~~even yourself when~~ your a piece of writing

95

feeling ~~too~~ *pushing*

is well-received, but more often than not, ~~experiencing~~ the familiar ~~bristling~~ *slush* and ~~incompleteness~~ ~~that~~

of inadequacy/when you ~~deliver~~ finish *a* report, *an* essay, article or examination.

Your uneasiness

~~foreboding~~ is ~~of course~~ usually confirmed when ~~the~~ *your* boss or teacher comments

completed

on what you have ~~done~~: "Good start, ... *NoT bad* Shows promise . . . . There are

or "Too bad you didn'T have more Time"

indications that . . . ," You know the phrases. You've heard them often.

adhere to ~~enforce~~ "This basic law) I doubt if you'll

similar *again* If you understand and ~~follow the instructns of this book,~~ you'll never again

hear/comments, ~~in~~ like ~~those mentioned above~~. Begin by reading and rereading ~~this law,~~

~~practice~~ play with it a little to see how it ~~works~~ *operates*

~~this basic law,~~ then memorize it. From now on, whenever you write anything

obey This law.

(except, perhaps, love letters — but it might even work then, too), ~~follow it~~

(depending upon what your ...)

~~in sequence.~~

Another glorious mess! Each time I would reread it in preparation for the day's writing, I would make some small changes—a word here, a sentence there. Finally, with the completed rough draft of this book in front of me, I settled in for serious revision—with the result that I decided to rewrite this revised first page. Compare page 1 of *Writing From Scratch* with the above revised draft.

You should use a similar procedure in everything you write, and you must know the difference between *revising* and *rewriting*. In the note on writing under pressure, I showed you what minor revisions are: the addition of specific examples, the changing of a few words, the sharpening of sentences, the correcting of errors. The above draft of page 1 shows more extensive revisions.

When you rewrite, however, you start with a fresh sheet of paper, and even though you use many of your original ideas and illustrations, you write an entirely new draft which must itself then be revised.

To create final copy for your project, to insure that impeccable, thumbprint-free, professional-looking manuscript with which you hope to dazzle your reader, you must revise and rewrite your rough draft so that except for the way the page looks, the words on your revised draft are almost identical to those which will appear on your final copy.

Note the word "almost." As with every step in the writing process, even the act of writing final copy from a revised draft will cause some changes—*but not many.* If you find yourself making major alterations at this stage of writing, realize that you are not writing final copy but merely another revised draft—which will need further work.

Much like the Topic limiting process, the act of revising never really stops. William Butler Yeats, for example, kept rereading copies of his own published works, poems which had gained him the reputation of being one of the world's great poets. Since his death, scholars have shown that Yeats was revising even those published poems which had already won international praise.

There are some basic concepts and techniques which make the process of revision more effective. First, you should always revise *in context.* When you change, add, or delete, make certain that you know how a particular revision will affect other parts of your essay. If you decide to change point of view, for instance, calling the reader "you" as I am doing here, be certain that you make that change throughout. Don't leave phrases such as "a reader" or "for example, a student's writing . . ." unless you definitely mean to do so. One of the best examples I know of failure to revise in context can be seen in Hemingway's *The Old Man and the Sea* (Scribner's, 1952). Literary critics have made much of the symbolic value of the number three which appears often in this novel, and the old man Santiago's *three* fishing lines form part of this symbol complex. Unfortunately, both Hemingway and his proofreaders apparently failed to revise one number on the final draft. On one page, Santiago's *four* lines are mentioned. Read *The Old Man and the Sea* (it's a great book). Practice your proofreading skills. Find this numerical oversight in Hemingway's only slightly flawed masterpiece.

Second, when you start revising your first draft, look at the *whole* essay. Don't *read* it yet; *look* at it—and make some notes. Is each section, each paragraph basically the same size as the others? Is there one section in which you have written much more than in another? If so, does this section come at the end (Ascending Importance)? If not, is your lack of balance intentional and effective? When revising, some writers actually copy their outline numbers and letters on their rough drafts, just to check for balance. I am not suggesting that you strive to make the paragraphs of your essays resemble a string of equally sized sausages, but whenever your rough draft *looks* unbalanced, you must know why—and make the decision whether to change or retain the unbalanced sections. Often, when you see a long draft paragraph surrounded by a number of shorter ones, you should assume that you can split the long one or combine two or three of the shorter ones. Usually, however, you'll find that an overly long paragraph either contains many more specific illustrations than the others do, or that you're using too many words to say something relatively simple.

Third, once you determine that your draft *looks* balanced, check each paragraph's opening sentence. Does this sentence in some way point back to the preceding paragraph? Reread the beginning sentence of this paragraph. See how the word "Third" and the phrase "your draft *looks* balanced" continue the ideas mentioned earlier? This device is known as Transition, and proper transitions between paragraphs (and within paragraphs among sentences and illustrations) make the reader's job much easier. If you have organized properly, transitional phrases will seem to come naturally, and if omitted on the rough draft, they can easily be inserted during revision. If you cannot achieve good transitions in your opening sentence, however, your organization is faulty. Even though you like what a paragraph says, get your scissors ready. The entire paragraph may have to be moved.

Finally, during this initial look at your manuscript, if you see the need for additional material, usually in the form of added specific examples, write a note to yourself in the appropriate margin (see page 81 for this kind of note on my rough draft). You'll want to add those additional examples during the reread-ing and intensive revising process. I've made comments to myself such as "need more facts," "doubtful," and "unjustified" during my initial looks at drafts.

Then, start rereading and revising. I'd suggest using a pencil for this process, because as usual, you are going to change your mind. Often, as I have for this book, you will cross out sentences or phrases which you don't like, then decide that perhaps they aren't so bad after all. Revising in ink often obliterates. You'll also revise words and phrases by adding new ones which may not be much better, and you'll want to refine them further. You can always erase pencil marks.

Start by reading your introduction, then your conclusion. Do they relate to each other? Does your introduction really introduce—or does it just mechanically state, "Here is what I'm going to say, dear reader, and here is my thesis statement which sums everything up." How many similarly patterned, dull introductions have I read! An introduction should engage the reader's attention, should give that reader a *reason* for continuing farther into your paper. If you state all your points in capsule form, *most* readers will stop there, even though you may have presented a startlingly new idea. Your boss may buck your paper for evaluation to another division; your instructor will think "Here we go again"; and all you have done is diminish the overall impact of all your work. An introduction points *toward;* it does not summarize (that is the purpose of an abstract, a short summary which is required for many professional papers). After all, you have sweated over every word of that paper—and you want your audience to read each one.

The best way to learn what an introduction should do is to look at any national magazine (do so the next time you're standing in line at the supermarket) and examine the opening paragraphs of each article. Certainly you have access to one such publication. Go get it. Read only the opening paragraphs. For example, I have reached for an issue of the *Dartmouth Alumni Magazine* (a dangerous venture, I think. What if my idea doesn't work? I'm stuck with using it as an example, though). Here are some of the introductory paragraphs:

(1) To ascertain how well it is doing the job it professes to do, the Alumni College is turning an introspective gaze on its own purposes and procedures and is soliciting comments and suggestions from other alumni.

(2) When Mike Colacchio '80 composes a poem, he presents it in style. For the presentation of one in particular, he donned long pink ears and a fuzzy white tail.

(3) During a recent conversation about the teaching of ethics at Dartmouth, an administrator at the College recounted an incident that occurred his freshman year, sometime in the late fifties: . . . .

(4) Orville Rodberg has never been to Hanover. Mention Dartmouth, however, and he'll see green, all right. Orville is a real
estate agent . . . in West Palm Beach.

(5) Swimming at Dartmouth has become a family affair, and it
frequently leaves coach Ron Keenhold scratching his head. "In
my 20 years at Dartmouth, two brothers on the same team
would be something. Having three sets of siblings on the team
this winter is a very unusual circumstance," notes Kennhold.

If you'll examine these five introductory paragraphs for essays
whose subjects range from athletics to ethics, you can see that
none of them tells you what the essay is going to *say,* but you do
have an idea what the essay is going to be *about*—and they
introduce their topics by using one of the standard introductory
devices: an anecdote, a direct quotation, a provocative statement,
an allusion, or the statement of a problem. No matter what your
Limited Topic, your introduction should create a need for the
reader to continue—and as I've mentioned before, you can never
write a satisfactory introductory paragraph before finishing your
draft. Plan to sweat a lot over those opening words.

Similarly, by revising your conclusion as the next step, you will
be accomplishing two necessary tasks: first, because you have just
looked at your introduction, you'll be able to insure that your final
words, phrases, and ideas relate to and even echo those with
which you began, in effect justifying the promise of your introduction. Second, by having your conclusion firmly in mind as you
revise the body of your essay, you can force the reader, often
without him or her knowing it at the time, to anticipate your
conclusion. You'll also build the threads of coherence which will
hold your work together.

Here are the conclusions to two of the articles noted above:

(3) The academic concern for ethics is a contemporary expression
of the College's original goals, [the Associate Dean] added.
"We're trying to move back toward the model of a college
where moral philosophy is integrated in all its activities."

(4) I *did* come back with the best tan of my life and 15 pounds
lighter. I even managed to exercise a little self control and put
aside a nice bundle of cash. But I'm fairly confident I won't be
renting from Orville Rodberg again in the near or distant
future.[1]

[1]*Dartmouth Alumni Magazine* (March, 1981), *passim.*

Because each of these conclusions echoes its introduction, a reader feels a sense of completion—and the writer's points have been much better made. The other articles just dribbled off—their promise unfulfilled.

After doing some preliminary revision on both introduction and conclusion, stop. Ask yourself one question. How well does the approximate length of your draft compare with your original intention? If you know that your audience (your boss, *Esquire* magazine, your instructor) has requested or usually likes writing projects of a certain length, or if you had decided to write just so many pages, you should now evaluate your interim achievement.

If you've organized and developed well, your draft will probably be too long. For my sample essay, I want no more than 4000 words; my draft, however, now runs about 5400 words. How do I know? By counting words on three randomly selected lines, then multiplying by the average number of lines, then by the number of draft pages. *Don't* count words as you write. Doing so interrupts and slows down your writing. I know that cutting my essay by 1000 words should be no problem, but those last 400 are going to vanish reluctantly. Depart they must, however, as should quite a bit of your first draft work. No one writes well the first time through.

If you think that your rough draft seems too short, your problem may be that you have not included enough specific illustrations. A good general rule is that the greatest part of an essay should be illustration, supported by details. Here is a paragraph from *The Elements of Style,* the brilliant book by William Strunk Jr. and E. B. White. The subtopic of this illustrative paragraph is the language of advertising, and you should note the circled specific examples the authors use to make their point that one should "prefer the standard to the offbeat":

> Today, the language of advertising enjoys an enormous circulation. With its deliberate infractions of grammatical rules and its crossbreeding of the parts of speech, it profoundly influences the tongues of children and adults. Your new kitchen range is so revolutionary it *obsoletes* all other ranges. Your counter top is beautiful because it is *accessorized* with gold-plated faucets. Your cigarette tastes good like a cigarette should. And, like the man says, you will want to try one. You will also, in all probability, want to try writing that way, using that language. You do so at your peril, for it is the language of mutilation[2] (Emphasis added.)

[2]*William Strunk Jr. and E. B. White, The Elements of Style,* revised edition, New York: Macmillan, 1979, p. 82.

Notice how the paragraph's main idea is developed by specific, sensuous examples: the kitchen range, the counter top, the cigarette accompany the specific words *"obsoletes," "accessorized,"* and *"like"* that themselves illustrate the point about the improper language of advertising. As do most good writers, Strunk and White practice what they preach, and they use more illustration than explanation in their writing. So too should you, and if your draft seems a bit shorter than you might like, fill it out with more specific examples.

Throughout this revision process, look for specifics, specifics, specifics. Recognize your good illustrations; improve the poor ones by making the reader *see*. Not only with examples such as counter tops and ranges, but with every word as well: strive for the specific instead of the general. In the above example, the final sentence could have read, "Don't write this way, for it is not right," and the same general meaning would have been presented. What a difference, however, is achieved by the use of the more specific words "peril" and "mutilation"!

In general, you should develop a revision process which best fits *you*. After writing a few papers or reports, you should be able to recognize most of your drafting peculiarities. Do you use overly abstract words? Do you have difficulty sticking to one idea per paragraph? Do you tend to go off on peripheral tangents? Does your spelling need work? Do you write simple, repetitive sentences? Do you misuse words? Do you sprinkle your prose with the flavorless word "thing"? Do you often promise more in the beginning of a project than you deliver at the end? Do you use certain words and phrases such as "on the other hand" and "but" over and over again? Do you have difficulty with specific grammatical constructions? These mistakes are common, but each writer usually demonstrates a particular and personal pattern of errors. Discover what your pattern is—then look for it when you revise. After a while, you will begin to anticipate your own problems and solve some of them before the fact, thus further improving the quality of your first draft prose.

Revision, then, is a systematic, often grueling process. Here in summary is what you should consider every time you start revising:

OVERALL BALANCE
INTRODUCTION AND CONCLUSION: Balance and
    echo?

TRANSITIONS
SPECIFIC ILLUSTRATION AND LANGUAGE: Development and examples?
SENTENCES: Grammar, style, variety? Words and ideas repeated unintentionally?
TYPOGRAPHICAL, SPELLING, AND OTHER HASTY ERRORS.

I have been dreading this next task. I hate to revise. I'll present selections only, but what will follow should, I hope, demonstrate how I do it, a method which you can use as a model for your own work. I am going to pick up my sharpened pencils, find my scissors and tape, get a clean yellow pad, pour a cup of coffee, and move away from this uncomfortable typing chair into the living room. Perhaps a change of scene will help me achieve the total objectivity needed for an excellent revision. *Total* objectivity? Well—perhaps *some* objectivity, at least.

Revision and Proofreading Symbols

In order to revise properly, you should know how to use some standard methodology. You will see how I use these symbols on the pages which follow. Most typists and all editors know them.

letter, word or,

Omission. Add appropriate phrase.

Transpose letters (words or.)

When you decide, ~~irrevocably and finally~~ to cut ~~out dumb irrelevancies out of~~ your, ~~otherwise impeccable~~ prose, indicate ~~what~~ final version ~~is to be~~ like this.

Begin new parapgraph. When you use this mark, typist will indent on new line.

Delete punctuation where pigtail line ends.

Add appropriate punctuation where indicated, Its similar to the first symbol.

Underline those few words you just <u>have</u> to italicize, such as book titles: <u>Moby Dick</u>.

Circle comments or instructions that you do <u>not</u> want to appear in your final manuscript.

use capital letter here.

Use lower case letter here.

Delete letter and close up.

Divide words which have been inadvertantly run together.

Time: two working hours later. (Total time so far for my essay: 6 hours, 18 minutes.)

Scene: *Writing from Scratch* author wishing he could drop entire project and go fishing.

Reason: Revision always hurts. Always.

You'll recall that I mentioned earlier how you must overcome the feeling that your words on paper seem to be so much a part of you that chopping away at them often seems impossible. The pain, I think, results not only from the fact of your having created those words, but also because it is just as unpleasant to recognize that you have written poorly as it is to accept your own children's real failings. Reading your rough draft is much like discovering that your son has stolen and sold a neighbor's bicycle.

I have not finished my revisions, but it is time to stop and comment on what I have done so far—and why.

First, after looking at the draft, I made the following notes:

INTRO —

Return to wife at end — balance —

Development / Balance OK — —
  But first part seems too long

Need to add more winks? More
"not really 's"?

  Add to last conversation:
    ① her getting up enough nerve
    to come over —
        I was a "woman" man.
    ② how she felt at end —

    ③
  Account for short story's writing — pp 24

Too long —

After checking for transitions (I noticed and marked a bad one on draft page 10, p. 72 of *Writing from Scratch*), I worked on the introduction and conclusion. Here are these two pages.

INTRODUCTION:

~~We were parked on the side of Route 55 south of Fairfield, Conn.~~
It was over there, I told my wife, where Marian's house ~~was was~~
had been

~~My wife~~
~~She said that she couldn't see anything. The~~ maple and oak ~~trees were too thick.~~

I remembered as
~~It in what~~ ~~had been been~~ a vacant field. This must be the corner, I thought,

~~Even though what used to be a small,~~ ~~white framed~~ dirty-white frame
There was only a shining, red and white
~~Mobil Station station was now a Self~~ self-serve AMOCO convenience store where
my Mobil Station had been. "Over there," I told my wife,
once
~~Everything was so much more open, I told my wife, when I worked there. She~~
was Marian's house, behind the thick maple and oak
said that she knew. I had told her the story ~~today~~ about Marian, she ~~didit~~
trees which filled what had been an empty field. My
added. ~~About the only~~ ~~similarity~~ familiar feeling July was the heat which made both of us feel
wife said she couldn't see it. Neither could I.
sticky.

my house?   My wife   that's why
"Want to see ~~where I used to live~~," I asked. ~~txxx~~ ~~She~~ said sure, ~~why~~
we came, wasn't it?
especially   though.
~~not.~~ She didn't want to see Marian's house, ~~xxxxxxx~~. We were running late.

large   now
~~Because~~ trees ~~xxxxxxxxxxxx~~ shielded the sign, I missed the turnoff

I had taken every day that summer x when I walked home from work. I made
a U-turn, then found the road on which I had once lived.
right
~~Ixxxxxxxxxxxxxxxxxxxxquixxxxxxxand this time found the road. Therexx~~

summers
~~Thirty-three~~ ~~years~~ before, ~~Ixxxxxxx~~ a slightly plump fifteen-year-old,
started
I had ~~found~~ my first regular job as a gas station attendant, and shortly

after that, I had met and fallen in love with Marian. Pumping -----------

~~Conclusion~~
Conclusion

The next day, we said all those damned goodbyes, and I
haven't seen her since.

Marian too, I know now, ~~felt~~ felt just as unrequited as I had, and

for ~~xxxx~~ many of the same reasons. She had been as obsessed with me as I had

been with her, ~~she had felt the similar twinges when we had so~~

~~unpredictebly met;~~ and she ~~xxxxxx~~ too ~~xxxxxx~~ believed that everything

had worked out for the best, that our mutual first love had helped us ~~xxxx~~

do more than just grow up. We exchange Christmas cards now; our children

are ~~xxxxxxx~~ starting familes of their own; and we have no regrets.

~~Well, I suppose — As~~ Marian would say, not really.

Then, resharpening my pencils, I attacked the body of the essay. When I revise, especially when I know that there should be some substantial cuts made, I do so in two ways. First, I work through the entire draft looking for large chunks (phrases, sentences, entire paragraphs) that can be excised or substantially condensed. I ask myself as I read, "Are these words absolutely necessary, or did I perhaps get carried away and write material that even though interesting, just doesn't fit?"

Also, I look for any opportunity to tighten my prose, to make one or two words do what five or even ten had done on the rough draft. In a relatively long essay such as this one, I know that there will be repetitions and contradictions which must also be changed.

Of course, I correct errors and make other changes as I go along, and now the pages of my draft all now look like the ones which follow.

Pumping gas was not my idea of a career, but I needed the money. I
had walked into the two pumps peeling Mobil Station, the week
previous, and asked the old man who was alone inside
the spotted glass case if he needed some help. He looked about 75
he was wearing a stained trainman's cap, and needed a shave. "Can't pay
much," he said. "You a mechanic?" I told him I knew a little about engines.
"You got working papers?" I told him I was fifteen.

"Can't even pay that much then," he said. We settled on an hour. I
would start the next day for a week's trial. "Then I'll see," he

I started work the next day.
Usually, all I did was pump gas, check and add oil, and
change a few tires. I was Mr. Simms' first hired man, and he seemed to take
little interest in me. His pumps were the pre World War II kind with the
glass bubbles on top, and there was no hydraulic lift, in the one
car bay, a pit which was slippery from what I suspected was
a thirty-year accumulation of oil pan drippings.
Inside the tiny "office" the glass display case contained some
which filled half of the tiny "office" was an assortment of old candy bars, rusty
cans of oil additive, some of which were rusted on top, some fan belts, some
car waxes whose labels I had never seen before, and a few roadmaps of
Maine, North Carolina, and other faraway places.

On my first day, Mr. Simms left for "lunch" at noon. He did not

On this page, my revisions attempt to correct drafting habits
that I know I possess: wordiness, repetition, irrelevancies, and
boring simple sentences.

Statements such as "my idea of a career" and "a thirty-year
accumulation of oil pan drippings" are too cute and have no place
in this essay. The original second sentence, among others, was a

compound sentence (two main clauses connected by a conjunction, here, "and"), the weakest kind of sentence one can write. By turning this sentence into a *complex* sentence (making one clause dependent upon the other), I established time and also achieved better focus on the old man, to whom this paragraph belongs. Similar emphasis resulted when I changed the third sentence from a simple series to a complex construction. Most good writers agree: in conventional, expository prose, complex sentences are more powerful. If you refuse to use complex constructions, . . . (see what I mean? By starting this sentence with the subordinating word "if," I forced you to anticipate what I was leading up to), you'll write boring prose. Strive for sentence variety, but whenever possible, revise by making many of your sentences complex.

Finally, in line two, I changed "two-pump, paint peeling" to "nearby," because I didn't like the clumsy alliteration,[3] and I wanted to keep the focus on the old man. I made this revision, however, *after* I had decided to add "two old gas" to line three of the second paragraph. This paragraph presents the gas station spatially, taking the reader from the pumps to the bay to the interior, where the glass case is first mentioned. I realized here that this case will become central to my essay as it is first cleaned, then is leaned upon by Marian, then becomes spotted again. Incidentally, when writing the rough draft I did not intend to emphasize this display case—but while revising, I decided that it would work nicely as a descriptive focal point.

The next draft page demonstrates a different kind of revision: the wholesale slaughter. When preparing this page for final typing, I intend to scissor out the entire midsection. I realized that I had already established that there had been "only six customers" while Mr. Simms was at lunch, and I remembered that I did in fact do a few oil changes and grease jobs. Perhaps, too, my first thoughts about why I had been hired had been after-the-fact speculation. Although the anecdote about the livery stable sounded good when I wrote it, the story may or may not be true. So I chopped away, achieving more tightness and saving about 150 words.

[3] I haven't forgotten. Use your dictionary.

~~to~~ return until ~~almost~~ 1/2 past four. ~~Idont~~ There had been only ~~four~~ six customers, *and)*

~~I think, and two or three others who had stopped for to ask directions.~~

~~in the threadbare arm chair~~
~~No~~ problems, I told my obviously beery boss. He sat ~~down~~ behind the ~~glass~~

display case. "Good," he said. "Go home. Se you in the morning." ~~I wondered~~
~~since.~~

~~If he noticed, knockknxxxkkkxx that I He could see through the glass.~~

Most of the days were similar ~~to that first one.~~ ~~Very little~~
~~business.~~ *very, very slow, I wondered how we.*
~~business. Just enough, I calculated, to pay fxxxxxxxxxxxxx my wages and~~

~~leave about an equal amount for Mr. Simms.~~ Occasionally, such as on the

July 4th holiday weeked, we would see a rush —but usually there would be

only four or five customers an hour, none of whom seemed "regular." ~~Mrxfimms~~

There were no ~~IxxgIxxxxIxxxx~~ appointments for grease jobs or oil changes,

no requests for tuneups or tires — just gas, and off the customer would go.

~~Acbt the only regularity was the lngth of Mr. Simms's lucnh hour — and~~

it was not long beofre I realized that the major reason he had hired me was

to give himself a break from the chores, he once told me, he had been doing

sold his livery stable in 1921.
since he had ~~xxxxxxxxxxxxxxxxxxxxxxxxx~~
Simms could afford me — but because I needed the job, I never asked. With so much)
~~Consequently, I had~~ time on my hands, ~~so I~~ ~~I xxxxt~~ began cleaning up the

station, inside and out. I pulled ~~xxxxx~~ the weeds which had come from the
which were since new
three acre ~~vacant lot~~ *open field* to the north, ~~kxkxxx~~ ~~which were a~~ beyond which I could ~~see a few~~ *nwer houses.)*

~~through the trees.~~ I shined the ~~xx~~ pumps and mowed the small island between
patched   straightening up
the asphalt ~~of the~~ apron and the raod. I began ~~starighetning~~ up the

Although similar revisions disfigure each succeeding page, on draft page 7 (pages 69–70 of *Writing from Scratch*) I noticed a different kind of problem: lines 13 and 14 contain the statement, "I don't recall ever seeing my brother or sister," yet I told the story later in the paper of my sister's snicker at the dinner table. Out went the contradiction, along with some overly sophomoric prose:

every day, ~~shortly after Mr. Simms would leave.~~ ~~Shxxxxxdxxxxdxxx~~

~~MXX~~ Mr. Simms's From her side porch she could see ~~hxx xxx~~ 1939 Ford chug ~~its way xx~~ away

~~down the Route 35 toward Ridgefield,~~ and within half an hour, there she would

be, usually dressed in shorts, sometimes with her shirt tied halter

fashion, often ~~with~~ carrying a paper bag with her lunch (and sometimes a

sandwich for me). Occasionally, she would bring a book which she would read

while I was outside, trying to concentrate on my job.

     That summer, I saw Marian at least six days a week. ~~SXXXXXXXXXXXXXX~~

On Mondays and Tuesdays, we would swim, bicycle somewhere for a picnic,

or play tennis (she wanted to learn -- to have me teach her). ~~At a nearby~~

~~court.~~ Some days, we would spend the afternoon or evening at each others' houses,

with our mothers always present but (obviously) not visible. We would read, listen to

the radio, or talk. ~~That summer, I don't recall ever seeing my brother~~

~~or sister, nor do remember doing anything with my parents. Everything was~~

~~Marian, Xxxxxxxxxxxx such was my obsession with her.~~ After about a month,

we confessed our love for each other, and ~~xx~~ I knew that ~~what we had~~

~~together was irrevocable, permanent, and unique.~~ No one had ever loved

anyone   as strongly or as completely as I did Marian.

     Of course, we did more than talk. We fumbled, touched, kissed,

explored, ~~xxxxxxxxx~~ nibbled, and seemed forever trying to catch our

The next page indicates a return to the slaughterhouse, and
here, I became slightly ashamed of myself. The entire central
paragraph is just so much wishful thinking, and I cannot imagine
any reader doing much more than snicker the way my sister did.
By attempting to attach cause to our breathless continence, I may

have been making us more "responsible" than we really were. We didn't because we didn't, and anyway, such an examination of psychological motives seems out of place in this essay. Out with it. (This revision hurt, though. Wouldn't all of us like to be able to understand exactly *why* we do what we do? Oh well, some other time.)

Also, the comment about the drivers' license violates temporal development, so I decided to move it to a later point. As you'll see, however, after some reflection I threw this sentence out as well.

breaths. We used the word "frustration" a lot, and I learned how

to say "No!" with ~~sharp yearning~~ fatalistic yearning. Once, when

we thought my parents were out for the entire evening, we went upstairs to my room,

but before anything could develop, the sound of tires in the gravel driveway

brought us racing down the steep stairs, just in time. My mother had forgotten

her purse. We never went upstairs again. ~~We decided that to try that again would be too risky.~~

In August, I received my drivers' license -- and whenever I could pry

my father's car loose, Marian and I transferred our ~~fuckings~~ breathlessness seat to the front (never in back, she said). That we always "stopped," I think,

was a result of fear, ignorance, and what we did not recognize then as

a ~~growing~~ budding sense of responsibility. We were afraid, of course,

of ~~pregnancy~~; we were ignorant, basically, of not what to do but of exactly

how to do it; but most important, we did have a sense that a

complete sexual relationship carried with it some responsibilities that we

were not, despite our feeling so mature, ready to handle. I think now,

looking back, that we really liked each other. Perhaps that fact was

the reason that we preferred frustration to consummation.

Althought our world consisted of each other, I could not help

Here's another revised page. I decided that the episode of the short story was irrelevant, as was the perhaps pompous assertion that I now understand more about my wife's reaction. Like the time spent in the rough draft talking about Mr. Simms's motivation, to mention my wife's possible motivation here would distract the reader from the central focus—Marian and me. So I decided to stick to the facts. When revising your own work, you do so too.

noticing some [outside] reactions ~~from many other people~~. Mr. Simms, for instance,

suggested>
~~told me~~ late one afternoon that   (STOP 11:30)   sT...

wheeled a loaded cart around a corner and collided with an extremely

pregnant woman who just shook her head at me and smiled. "You're still

bumping into things, aren't you," she said. It was Marian, ~~carrying she~~

~~told me later as we talked in the parking lot, her fourth child.~~ Her
[she told me in the parking lot,]

husband, was a student pilot in ~~another~~ [the] squadron ~~which worked opposite hours~~
~~in which~~   [He and Then] ~~and~~ would be graduating in a month.>
~~to the one I was instructing.~~ We would have to get together, she said,

to talk about old times.

/We never did. That night, ~~at home,~~ [when I told her about ~~whatever~~] with my wife ~~wondering what~~

~~on earth was the matter,~~ I started to write ~~again, this time~~ a short

story ~~about a young man's first love.~~ ~~Thxxxx~~ I finished it three days

later, ~~and when I showed it to my wife~~ ~~and told them~~

~~what had caused this creative resurgence,~~ [my wife] said only that she ~~didn't~~

~~think she~~ and Marian would have ~~much~~ [probably little] in common and ~~why~~ anyway, hadn't

I said that instructors and students should [not] mingle socially? ~~As with~~

~~my relationship with Marian, I think I understand more now~~ [about my wife] ~~than I did~~

~~then, but~~ I realized ~~that at least~~ that pressing for a reunion would at least

```
                                decided to bring up the subject
be difficult, and by the time I brought up the subject again, Krejen's
                                                            Marian's

husband had already graduated and had been assigned to Germany.  I had

of course checked with instructor friends of mine in his squadron.  He was

a good guy and a good pilot.  I felt happy for her.
```

As I neared the end of this draft revision exercise, I began to feel more intense pressure. After all, the last paragraphs of an essay are often the reason for writing the piece in the first place. Still concerned with specifics, tighter sentences, and proper word choice, I referred to my earlier notes about the last conversation. In draft form, this section seemed flatter than I wanted it to be; there were not enough details of what we said. So I added some. Note how the small but rather significant change of "near past" to "future" (line 9) better introduces what the paragraph is really about.

```
                    without reading it.
one which followed  Yes, she had watched me for the first two weeks of
      next
the following summer, and had been coming over when she heard about
                              thinking of

Anne — who was so much prettier than she was.  I disputed that, and
                                                            and in a word
     She had been so nervous that first day. I seemed so mature/she
we laughed some more. Yes, that night when my mother came back  thinking at,)
                                    The
( I really laughed at that one.)
unexpectedly had been terrifying.  No, she had not been as close to an

she had been with me with with anyone else until after we broke up.

No, I had never told her about Mr. Simms' remark about the
     She still had no idea what had so infuriated me that I wrote
lipstick. And on, and on, and on.    the letter. . I said
                        nothing, even then, about her
                        imagined kissing.

We also talked about the present and near past, about our families,
                        future
our children (we each had fifteen-year-olds who were exhibiting the same
                                                    similarly
silly symptoms just as we had), and our general mistakes and fears.
                                                    Her
                                                    Thought
        today's                                      .       had been
We agreed that given the standards of today, our relationship was
```

really quite innocent, ~~and~~ but that despite our individual sense of

fr~~u~~stration at the time, really fun. ~~Not idyllic, but for the most part —~~

~~fun.~~ Most important, ~~XXXXXX~~ we agreed that our experience had served

to caution us <u>not</u> to interfere with our own children ~~when they~~ too ^is growing up. Our^
parents had done reasonably well; we would do better.
~~unnecessarily~~
~~Would talk so obviously foolishly~~ be experiencing those <u>first love</u>

~~depressions and fears,~~ ~~and~~ As I ~~fell~~ asleep, ^was feeling^ I remember Marian's
^in the chair^
hand and her last statement; "You know," she said," I really love my

husband." I told her that I really loved my wife. "But," she said,

"I love you too." "Me too," I said. Then I ~~fell asleep~~ dozed off.

Finally, I worked on the conclusion again. Note the reworking on the lower left.

The next day, we said all those damned goodbys, and I haven't seen her since.

Marian too, I know now, ^yet^ felt just as unrequited as I had, and

for ~~xxxx~~ many of the same reasons. She had been as obsessed with me as I had

been with her; ~~she had felt the similar twinges when we had so~~

~~unpredictebly met;~~ and she~~x~~ too ~~xxxxxxx~~ believed that everything

had worked out for the best, that our ~~m~~utual first love had helped us ~~xxxx~~

do more than just grow up. We exchange Christmas cards now; our children

are ~~growing~~ starting familes of their own; and we have no regrets. Come to

Think of it, my wife has never told me the
details of her "first love" — but it doesn't
~~Well — I suppose — as~~ Marian would say, not really ...

matter. On a future trip, I wouldn't
want to be particularly interested at all.
in seeing his house, either.
What was — just was. No, it
doesn't really matter. Not really.
at all...

After finishing this revision yesterday, I mowed the lawn, then sprayed the garden for grasshoppers, an action which seems just as futile as trying to write a reasonably good essay. Contrary to what you might think, few writers really like to write—so you are no exception at all. Most professionals write because it's all they compulsively know how to do with some degree of satisfaction, but that satisfaction almost never comes *while* writing. As happened during the creation of my own rough draft, when you're pouring out words easily, you're probably composing either irrelevancies or just plain junk.

Look back over my revised draft pages in this chapter and attempt to see why I made each change. Compare the original draft with the revised version. Some of my revisions, I know, seem less needed than do others, and I'm not satisfied yet. What I'll have to do now is clean up the copy, literally cut out the slaughtered paragraphs, use a broad felt tip pen to obliterate those sentences that I have lined through, and rewrite or at least retype some of the pages which I have virtually destroyed by making so many changes.

Then, I'll take another look at the manuscript and do my final revisions. Using the same procedure as with my first revision, I'll create a final revised draft that will be ready for the typist. Hanging over me, however, is an extremely dark cloud: my rough estimate is that I'm still about 500 words over my stated limit. What's 500 words? Two manuscript pages? Why worry? Consider this scenario: for an important sales conference, your boss wants a presentation handout for three hundred delegates. "No more than three pages," he or she says menacingly. Are you going to give your boss *four* pages, thus requiring that someone else (probably the boss) do the cutting on the way to the airport? Of course not.

I won't either. What you will shortly see is the appropriately condensed, final version of my essay which now has the working title (I just this minute thought of it) "The Not-Really Summer Affair." I'm not entranced with this title, and it too will probably change.

A Final Note on Proofreading

Although the final task required for a writing project is proof-reading, you are actually proofreading all the time. Twice, how-ever, you should proofread intensely: first, when preparing your revised draft for typing; second, after your final draft has been completed.

Whenever you do your final proofreading, try to do the impos-sible: do not think about the content of your sentences. Look only at the words and the punctuation. Consider spelling, typographi-cal errors, and omissions. If possible, especially if you type your final draft yourself, wait as long as you can to do your proofread-ing, because the longer you wait, the more likely you are to forget exactly what is coming next; thus you'll be able to look freshly at each word and line.

Some professional proofreaders check final copy upside down and backwards; yet even with this attention to detail, some errors slip through. For my first book, a friend of mine and I spent two days proofreading; then the publisher's people went over it again. When I held the first printed copy tenderly in my hands, I could not help skimming—well, *reading* it. There were no misspellings, no typographical oversights, no composition errors. What we had all overlooked and omitted, however, was the first half of a most important poem.

Regardless, try to do the very best job of proofreading that you can, and realize that if you do overlook something, *that* error is what the reader of your paper will notice first and probably never forget. The more care you can devote to proofreading, the better overall impression your paper will create.

For example, I am going to leave a few *minor* errors in the final version of my essay that follows as Chapter 7. Look for them, and when you consider a writing project of your own to be perfect, remember the errors of mine that you just couldn't miss.

Chapter 8

The Summer "Not-really" Affair

═══════════════════════════════════════

I COULDN'T BELIEVE IT. What once had been my run-down Mobil station was now a glistening, red and white self-serve Amoco convenience store. The entire corner at the intersection of Routes 123 and 35 was asphalt. Thick maple and oak trees filled what had been a three-acre open field. Somewhere back in that forest, I told my wife, was Marian's old house. I used to be able to see it from where we were then parked.

The July New York State heat, at least, was the same, and I felt sticky. "Want to see where *I* lived?" I asked. My wife said sure, that's why we came, wasn't it? About wanting to see Marian's house, though, she said, "Not really." We were running late.

Because of the new growth, I missed the turnoff I had taken every day that summer thirty three years before; then I hardly recognized the house where I had lived. It seemed so much smaller than I remembered. "It's nice," my wife said. I thought of asking the occupants for a tour, but decided not to. We did have many miles to go that day.

Before all the trees too had grown up, I had been a slightly plump fifteen-year-old; and that summer I got my first regular job as a gas station attendant. Then I met and fell in love with Marian. In June, on a whim, I had walked into the cramped office of the tiny Mobil Station and peered down at the old man sitting behind the spotted glass display case. About 75, he was wearing a stained denim trainman's cap and needed a shave. "I want a job," I said. "Can't pay much," he said. "You a mechanic?" I said I knew a little about engines. "You got working papers?" I told him I was fifteen. "Can't even pay *that* much then," he said. "Might use you, though." He offered 50 cents an hour. Mondays and Tuesdays off. A week's trial. Then he'd see.

I started work the next day. His two old gas pumps still had the opaque glass bubbles on top, and there was no hydraulic lift, only a one-car bay, a dark, greasy, slippery pit that felt damp and cool when I would change someone's oil. Inside the tiny "office," the glass display case contained some old candy bars, rusty cans of oil additive, a few fan belts, some unfamiliar car waxes, and about a dozen dusty roadmaps of Maine, North Carolina, and other faraway states.

On my first day, Mr. Simms left for "lunch" at noon, not to return until almost four. There had been only six customers and no problems, I told my obviously beery boss. He took his seat in the threadbare arm chair behind the display case. "Good," he said. "Go home. See you in the morning."

Most of the following days were similar: very, very slow. I wondered how Mr. Simms could afford me—but because I needed the job, I never asked. With so much time on my hands, I began cleaning up the station, inside and out. I pulled the weeds which had come from the three-acre open field to the north, beyond which were some new houses. I shined the pumps and mowed the small island between the patched asphalt apron and the road. I began straightening up the greasy pit, throwing out all pieces of metal that I could not recognize, uncovering a screwdriver or a wrench which I replaced in a crusty, gunmetal gray tool box which I also cleaned. I arranged fan belts by size along one wall, even though there were few of the most popular sizes. I swept, polished, dusted and rearranged, and finally, after half a dozen customer requests, I even bought some fresh candy bars from a wholesaler who happened to stop by. The Hershey,

Snickers, and Baby Ruth bars looked colorful through the now clear glass of the display case.

As I was admiring this arrangement, a female voice behind me said, "I'll take a Hershey bar, please." Startled, I turned and saw Marian for the first time. Medium length dirty blonde hair tied in a pony tail. Thin lips with bright red lipstick framing slightly crooked teeth. Man's white button-down shirt with rolled-up sleeves. Red shorts. Sneakers. About my age, I remember thinking. Because she was standing on the weedy dirt and I was one step up in the doorway, she seemed very short. "Hi," she said. "I'm Marian. I live over there." She pointed across the vacant lot. "I've been watching you." Then she winked.

I felt flushed. My heart pounded, and yes, I fell in love immediately. Chauffeured by someone's parent, I had taken girls to movies. I had played tennis with them. I had danced with them at boarding school parties. I had listened to my younger sister's friends giggling in her room long into the night. And I had traded boasts with my own friends about how much I knew about girls, but except for one clumsy kissing spree in the woods with a girl whose name I've forgotten, I was as ignorant about women as I now realize that most of my boasting friends were, too. Here, unannounced, unexpected, was a pretty girl who had said that she had been "watching me."

During Mr. Simm's three-hour lunch that day, we talked in that tiny office about music and books (she had just started *The Naked and the Dead,* which she said with a wink that she kept hidden under her bed because of the language). She did not play tennis, nor did she ski—but she loved to swim. I knew the best pool in the river. I tried to imagine her in a bathing suit. Movies? Of course. She had friends who could drive, and we could go up to Danbury where there was a new outdoor theatre. Another wink.

That first conversation, with me sitting in the old chair and Marian usually walking up and down on the other side of the display case (her red shorts were about the same color as the Baby Ruth wrappers) was one of the most breathless discussions I have ever had. She seemed so poised, so vivacious, so much in control, while I kept tripping over my tongue or clearing my throat, and once I even forgot the title of the movie that I had just admitted seeing three times. When the first customer interrupted my idyll by honking his horn angrily, I bolted out of the chair and banged my knee on the side of the glass case. Marian giggled. After that, Marian sat in the chair and I hovered by the door, knowing that if she were seated behind the case there was less chance of a customer's seeing her.

At about three o'clock, she got up, walked around to where I was standing, and put her hand on my arm. I tingled. "I'd better go," she said. "Old Simms might come back early." She really had been watching. "Goodbye," she said. "See you tomorrow." I asked her if she wanted her Hershey bar. "Not really," she said. Half way across the open field, she turned and blew me a kiss.

Thus my first love began—with a request for a candy bar—and it lasted for a year. Marian would come over almost every day. From her side porch she could see Mr. Simms's 1939 Ford chug away and within half an hour, there she would be, dressed usually in shorts, sometimes with her shirt tied halter fashion, often carrying a paper bag with her lunch (and sometimes a sandwich for me). Occasionally, she would bring a book which she would read while I was outside trying to concentrate on my job.

That summer, I saw Marian at least six days a week. On Mondays and Tuesdays, we would swim, bicycle somewhere for a picnic, or play tennis (she wanted to learn—to have *me* teach her). Some days, we would spend the afternoon or evening at each others' home with a parent always somewhere in the house. We would read, listen to the radio, or talk. That summer, everything was Marian. After about a month, we confessed our love for each other, and I knew that no one had ever loved anyone as strongly or as completely as I did her.

Of course, we did more than talk. We fumbled, touched, kissed, explored, nibbled, and seemed forever trying to catch our breaths. We used the word "frustration" a lot, and I learned how to say "No?" with fatalistic yearning. Once, when we thought my parents were out for the entire evening, we went upstairs to my room, but before anything could develop, the sound of tires in the gravel driveway brought us racing down the steep stairs, just in time. My mother had forgotten her purse. We never went upstairs again.

Although our world consisted of each other, I could not help noticing some outside reactions. Mr. Simms, for instance, suggested late one afternoon that I'd better check my face before the next customer came. In the cracked mirror of the station's only bathroom, I saw the lipstick on my left cheek. As I bolted by him, face averted and completely red, I wondered if he were smiling. He never said anything else; nor did he change his lunch schedule, but we were much more careful after that.

My parents, too, began to take notice. One evening after dinner, my mother asked me if I wanted to take the daughter of a friend of hers to a movie the following night. I said no. A few days later at breakfast, she told me that I was invited to a picnic which just happened to be on my next day off. I declined as well that obviously contrived, I thought then, opportunity. It also seemed to me that my mother stayed home more often, especially when I was not working.

Marian's parents also seemed to take more interest in our closeness. There were more evenings taken up with "family" matters, Marian told me, and her cousins often seemed to arrive unexpectedly on my days off. Once, she was gone for a week with her mother and father, and because they had never before taken a vacation together, we began to suspect a plot.

The greatest insult came one evening at dinner when my father, a brandy in hand, looked at his watch and asked me whether I was seeing "Cuddles" that night. My mother looked a bit stricken. My sister choked into her napkin. I glared at all of them, these people with whom I had to live but whom I suddenly hated. Obviously, they had been talking about us. "I don't know what you mean," I blurted pompously, then rushed from the table to pout for a while in the sanctity of my room.

My friends, too, seemed to disappear. Early in the summer, they'd call to set up a softball game, some tennis, some fishing, but my the middle of August, the calls became rare. I had declined too often. When I would see friends in town, they seemed nice enough, but distant. One day in front of the drugstore, three of them converged on me, and asked if I wanted to go camping the following Monday. "He can't," one said. "He's working." The other two smirked and shook their heads. "No, he's not," another said. "He'll be playing kissy-face with good old Marian." I tried to hit him, but someone caught my arm, and three of them walked slowly away, not looking back, leaving me alone on the hot street corner.

At the end of summer, before Marian and I had to go back to our respective schools, a hundred miles apart, I told her that of course we were going steady, weren't we, and that we would have to write a lot of letters and that it would be a lonely fall. I had just received my driver's license and we were parked somewhere after seeing a movie. Her hesitant reaction surprised me. She loved me, she said, she absolutely did, but no—we weren't going steady. Her mother wouldn't allow it. I exploded. What did parents know, I told her. Our business was our business. If she loved me, she'd go steady anyway. She drew back as far as she could on the seat, looked at me, and said slowly, "I just can't." We were as good as going steady, even if we weren't, she added.

That fall we wrote dozens of letters, each of us professing loneliness, frustration, and undying love. We would never date anyone else, we vowed. I didn't, although I did attend one or two school dances. Once, when a girl I'd just met suggested that we walk outside where it was cooler, I refused stiffly and told her that I was "committed." I now know that the particular angle her right eyebrow assumed was her acknowledgment that I was, at least for the moment, a real jerk.

When Christmas vacation started, I arrived home first and insisted upon meeting Marian's train. I remember calling her parents and announcing that I would pick Marian up, and I assumed that they would not be there. I was wrong then, too. As Marian stepped down from a rear passenger car, the fur collar of her coat barely covered by her new page boy haircut, I raced toward her, only to see her smile and wave and then throw her arms around her mother—before I could get to her. I was allowed to carry her suitcase to her father's car.

The next night (she had to be with her family, that first evening), I sensed a change. There was something about her, something about the way she talked, the way she tossed her shorter hair, the overall way she acted that was different. On our second date, another movie, I felt even more uneasy, and the third time we were together, I decided to ask her. I scratched for the right words, then blurted, "You kiss differently."

"I what?" she said.

"You kiss differently," I repeated.

She replied, somewhat diffidently, that she really didn't know what I meant, but *I* knew. I also knew *she* knew. I asked her if there was anyone else. She replied of course not, not really, and when I asked her what "not really" meant, she shrugged her shoulders and answered, "Nothing." Then she added, "Anyway, you kiss differently too. So what."

I don't remember what else we said that night, but I do know that the evening ended dismally. I saw her only once again that vacation (her parents took her skiing for a week and did not invite me), and with adolescent frenzy I called up everyone I had known, went to a number of parties, and generally tried not to feel sorry for myself. Our last date was a disaster—a party at which she seemed to know everyone, and more tragically, everyone seemed to know her. I observed her talking two or three times in corners of a room to other young men, one of whom was even a friend of mine, and I drank too much beer. I'm not certain whether I even kissed Marian goodnight.

When I returned to school, I fumed for some time. Obviously, Marian had lied to me. She had been dating all fall, I knew, sharpening her kissing skills. I had obviously been stupid all that previous summer, too. I had been just one of many. That's what my friend's phrase "good old Marian" meant. Perhaps one of *them* had even been *him*. What else had she done with them that she hand't done with me? What had she been doing all fall? With whom? How often?

My anger and jealousy lasted well into March, even though Marian and I exchanged a few letters which seemed just slightly cooler than before. She looked forward to the summer, she said, when she too could drive, and was I going to work at the gas station again? She couldn't wait.

I'll bet, I thought. And I fumed some more. Finally, in late March I wrote the letter that vented all my pent-up fury. It was about ten pages, I think, and I told her that our relationship was over unless she stopped lying to me, told me everything, and promised never to do it again.

I waited until the middle of April for the reply which never came. I tried to call her three times, but the girl at the desk of her dormitory always said that she was out. I wrote a follow-up letter, modifying my position graciously, I thought, and begging her to write. She never did.

In June, when I started work again at the gas station, Mr. Simms looked the same, the glass case had reacquired its blotched appearance, but there wew two new pumps. My anger and jealously had abated, but what I felt for the first two weeks was despair. I tried to call Marian, but twice her mother said that she did not want to come to the phone. The third time, when I insisted upon talking to her, Marian told me that we really shouldn't see each other, at least not for a while, that we should just be friends.

So I would go to the little Mobil Station each day, try not to look too often across the field where I knew *she* was, and clean, snip, polish and prune with a frenzy, wondering if she were watching. Then, during the third week of that summer vacation, I managed to fall quickly and just as irrevocably in love with another girl whose name I think was Anne.

So ended my first "affair." My family moved. I graduated from college, then joined the Air Force. I doubt if I even thought about Marian again.

Ten years after that summer, however, while shopping in the Base Commissary for my family which now included three small children, I wheeled a loaded cart around a corner and collided with an extremely pregnant woman who just shook her had at me and smiled. "You're still bumping into things, aren't you," she said. It was Marian. Her husband, she told me in the parking lot, was a student pilot in another squadron, not the one in which I was an instructor. He would be graduating in a month. We would have to get together, she said, to talk about old times.

We never did. That night, I told my wife about Marian. She replied only that she and Marian would probably have little in common and anyway, hadn't I said that instructors and students should not mingle socially? By the time I got enough nerve to bring up the subject again, Marian's husband had graduated and they had been assigned to Germany. I had of course checked with instructor friends of mine in his squadron. He was a good guy and a good pilot. I felt happy for her.

It was years later, after I had divorced and remarried, that Marian's husband, now a Major, was assigned to my department at the United States Air Force Academy. He stopped by my office and introduced himself. He knew all about me, he said. Marian had told him (I wondered how much), and as soon as they were settled, we'd get together.

We did. There were Department functions, an occasional small dinner party, a picnic or two—but somehow Marian and I never talked about the old days at all. I came to respect Marian's husband; and our wives became at least social, if not really close friends. Then Marian's husband was transferred again, and I did not see them for two years.,

The cause of our last meeting was the death of a very close mutual friend. Marian's husband called me. There had been an aircraft accident. We had both known Tony Dater as the prince that he was; and when I heard that he had been killed, I had to go. When I stepped into the 100 degree heat of Big Spring, Texas, there was Marian, standing on the concrete ramp below the aircraft's exit ladder just as she had stood by the gas station door, twenty-eight years before. She drove me to their house and we held hands and cried all the way. We would both miss Tony very much.

Later that night, after the exhausting process of handling affairs for the funeral, talking with Tony's family and friends, and meeting new arrivals, Marian and I stayed up nearly until dawn. Perhaps it was the emotional release afforded by the death of a friend or perhaps it was just time to do so, but we relived our summer and fall, day by day, incident by incident, and we laughted and cried and held hands, and talked and talked and talked. Marian's husband had gone to bed early; there was another friend sleeping on the living room couch just a few feet away from where we sat; but nothing disturbed us at all.

No, she said, she had not been going out with anyone else that fall—well, she said smiling the way she had so often, *not really*. Maybe a *few* times. Nothing serious. Hadn't *I* been dating? No? She was surprised. She thought I had. Yes, my nasty letter had hurt her very much, and she had thrown away the one which followed without reading it. Yes, she *had* watched me for the first two weeks of the next summer and had been thinking of coming over until she heard about Anne—who was so much prettier than she was. I disputed that, and we laughed some more. She had been so nervous that first day. I had seemed so *mature*, she thought. I really laughed at that. Yes, the night when my mother came back unexpectedly had been terrifying. No, she had not been as close with anyone else as she had been with me until after we broke up. No, I had never told her about Mr. Simms' remark about the lipstick. She still had no idea what had so infuriated me that I wrote the letter. I apologized, finally, for being dumb.

We also talked about the present and future, about our families, our children (we both had fifteen-year-olds who were exhibiting similarly silly symptoms), and our general mistakes and fears. We agreed that given today's standards, our relationship had been really quite innocent, but despite our individual sense of frustration at the time, fun. Most important, we agreed that our experience had served to caution us *not* to interfere unnecessarily with our own children's growing up. Our parents had done reasonably well; we would of course do better. As I was falling asleep on the rollaway bed, I remember Marian's hand and her last statement: "You know," she said, "I really love my husband." I told her that I really loved my wife. "But," she said, "I love you too." "Me, too," I said. Then I dozed off.

The next day, we said all those damned goodbyes, and I haven't seen her since.

Marian too, I know now, had felt just as unrequited as I did, and for many of the same reasons. She had been as obsessed with me as I had been with her, yet she too believed that everything had worked out for the best, that our mutual first love had helped us become more than just mature. We exchange occasional Christmas cards now; our children are starting families of their own; and we have no regrets. No regrets? As Marian might say, not really? No. I'm certain. Not really at all.

CONCLUSION

SO THERE'S THE ESSAY—from scratch to publication. I spent about ten hours conceiving, structuring, writing, and revising it. Did the typographical errors jump out at you? (See p. 123, line 28, "my"; p. 125, line 18, "hadn't," and line 37, "wew"; p. 126, line 16, "had," p. 127, line 17, "laughted.") I'll bet that you stumbled over a couple of them, at least—and so too will your boss or instructor notice even the smallest errors on your final copy. Is perfection possible? Well, not really, but it's worth striving for.

I think you should examine, too, how I changed the introduction and conclusion. These two parts of any essay are vital: the introduction causes the reader to continue; the conclusion gives him or her a sense of completion. Please remember, though, that neither the introduction nor the conclusion can be properly polished until you have finished (and I mean really finished) the body of your work.

What I've demonstrated to you is how one kind of essay, the personal narrative, is written "from scratch," but as I have said often in this book, the principles apply to *any writing task* at all. To conceive, direct, structure, write, and revise an essay is never easy, but if you'll follow the basic steps I've suggested, I'm certain that your future written work will not only reflect your increased confidence but will also provide you with much more satisfaction and success.

Appendix

Guides to even better writing

William Strunk, Jr. and E. B. White. *The Elements of Style*. Macmillan.
> Throughout its many editions, "Strunk and White" has been an indispensable companion for those who wish to learn correct usage and style. Should be on everyone's desk.

Jean Wyrick. *Steps to Writing Well*. 3rd Edition. Holt, Rinehart and Winston. 1986.
> An easily read, straightforward guide to various strategies for writing expository prose. Contains sample essays, exercises, and a short handbook.

Donald Murray. *Write to Learn*. Holt, Rinehart and Winston, 1984.
> An excellent reference for tips, advice, and strategies about the writing process.

Robert Scholes and Nancy R. Comley. *The Practice of Writing*. 2nd Ed. Martin's, 1985.
> A variety of writing exercises for specific audiences and purposes along with short professional samples of writing for imitation.

Stephen Reid. *College Writing: Purpose and Process.* Prentiss-Hall, 1988.

>Combines the writer's purpose and intent with strategies for inventing, organizing, and writing.

The following three texts are larger, more comprehensive rhetorics (some with handbooks) which are up-to-date references for a wide range of writing situations and problems.

Elizabeth Cowan Neeld. *Writing Brief.* Scott, Foresman and Company, 1986.

Rise B. Axelrod and Charles R. Cooper. *The St. Martin's Guide to Writing.* St. Martin's, 1985.

Janice Lauer and others. *The Four Worlds of Writing.* Harper and Row, 1985.

Index